THOMAS JEFFERSON, AMERICA, PLEASE LISTEN

Clifford Olsen

THOMAS JEFFERSON, AMERICA, PLEASE LISTEN

ISBN-13: 978-1536961386

ISBN-10: 1536961388

DEDICATION

To my sons, Tony;
Christopher, a John Adams defender;
and Sean.

To my Granddaughter, Lyla,
who I hope will learn that history is important
and that her family had much to do with it.

CONTENTS

ACKNOWLEDGMENTS

Being reminded that the conversation in my head, needs to come out on paper, my bride, Andrea has been a help all through this book. My friend Wayne Schenewerk assisted on some of the chapters. It is interesting that all three of us started as being Democrats, two conservative, and Wayne, a union liberal. As the Democrat Party moved away to Socialism, and Wayne learning to think what the values of our country are or should be, we all, ended up very similar in thought. I want to thank them both.

The footnote such as "#xxx" are from The Jeffersonian Encyclopedia, Edited by John P. Foley, Copyright 1900, by Funk & Wagnalls Company.

The footnotes with LOC, come from the Library of Congress digital website. Other footnotes are self-explanatory.

The names of places from which Jefferson wrote are abbreviated as follows, and the dates follow, so you may see from where and at what time in his life he wrote, the quote.

Albemarle, Va.	Alb.	New York	N.Y.
Annapolis	A.	Nismes,	Ns.
Baltimore	B.	Paris	P
Chesterfield, Va.	Ches.	Philadelphia	Pa.
Eppington, Va.	Ep.	Popular Forest, Va.,	P.F.
Fairfield, Va	F.	Richmond	R.
Germantown	G.	Tuckahoe, Va.	T.
London	L.	Washington,	W.
Monticello	M.	Williamsburg, Va.,	Wg.

In the quotations, the mark * * * indicates an omission in the text. Words not in the text, but supplied by the Jefferson Cyclopedia Editor or the author are, in all cases, enclosed within [brackets]. I did not change Mr. Jefferson's spelling, however I did make paragraphs for ease of reading.

PREFACE

THOMAS JEFFERSON, AMERICA, PLEASE LISTEN takes a look at modern day issues, and responds to the issues in the words of Thomas Jefferson. Jefferson, a fervent writer on issues, seems to have written about everything, and kept copies of his writings and correspondence. Having shelves of his writings, I find that the one item that he did not mention, was what he thought of Missouri's capital city, the City of Jefferson, my town, being named for him.

I desired the book to be a conversation on the issues of the day, although I am not a conversationalist, neither was Jefferson. Jefferson's comments are in an italics type. I thought it important for Jefferson to tell you about himself, the man, so you may understand Jefferson, the politician, the philosopher, the patriarch. I give this in the preface, because I believe it is good to know, but not necessarily required for the book. You may read it here or proceed to Chapter One. So here we go.......

As we bring out selections of your writings, we need to learn a little of your background, education and experiences to understand you and why your writings and experiences matter in today's world. I believe that we need to know a little about you, Thomas Jefferson, the person, to understand your thought process and your personal morals in developing your position on the issues of the day. How about providing us your general background before we get started on the issues?

I have sometimes asked myself, whether my country is the better for my having lived at all? I do not know that it is. I have been the instrument of doing the following things; but they would have been done by others; some of them, perhaps, a little better:

The Rivanna had never been used for navigation; scarcely an empty canoe had ever passed down it. Soon after I came of age, I examined its obstructions, set on foot a subscription for removing them, got an act of Assembly passed, and the thing effected, so as to be used completely and fully for carrying down all our produce.

The Declaration of Independence.

I proposed the demolition of the Church Establishment, and the Freedom of Religion. It could only be done by degrees; to wit, the Act of 1776, c. 2, exempted dissenters from contributions to the Church, and left the Church clergy to be supported by voluntary contributions of their own sect; was continued from year to year, and made perpetual 1779, c. 36. I prepared the Act for Religious Freedom in 1777, as part of the Revisal, which was not reported to the Assembly till 1779, and that particular law not passed till 1785, and then by the efforts of Mr. Madison.

The Act putting an end to Entails.

The Act prohibiting the Importation of Slaves.

The Act concerning Citizens and establishing the natural right of man to expatriate himself, at will.

The Act changing the course of Descents, and giving the inheritance to all the children, &c., equally, I drew as part of the Revisal.

The Act for Apportioning Crimes and Punishments, part of the same work, I drew. When proposed to the Legislature, by Mr. Madison, in 1785, it failed by a single vote. G. K. Taylor afterwards, in 1796, proposed the same subject; avoiding the adoption of any part of the diction of mine, the text of which had been studiously drawn in the technical terms of the law, so as to give no occasion for new questions by new expressions. When I drew mine, public labor was thought the best punishment to be substituted for death. But, while I was in France, I heard of a society in England, who had successfully introduced solitary confinement, and saw the drawing of a prison at Lyons, in France, formed on the idea of solitary confinement. And, being applied to by the Governor of Virginia for the plan of a Capitol and Prison, I sent him the Lyons *plan, accompanying it with a drawing on a smaller scale, betted adapted to our use. This was in June, 1786. Mr. Taylor very judiciously adopted this idea (which had now been acted on in Philadelphia, probably from the English model), and substituted labor in confinement, for the public labor proposed by the Committee of Revisal; which themselves would have done, had they been to act on the subject again. The public mind was ripe for this in 1796, when Mr. Taylor proposed it, and ripened chiefly by the experiment in Philadelphia; whereas, in 1785, when it had been proposed to our Assembly, they were not quite ripe for it.[1]*

You have been involved with science, agriculture, politics and education. Tell us more of the politics and education.

I came of age in 1764, and was soon put into the nomination of justice of the county in which I lived, and, at the first election following, I became one of its representatives in the Legislature. I was thence sent to the old Congress. Then employed two years with Mr. Pendleton and Mr. Wythe, on the revisal and reduction to a single code of the whole body of the British Statutes, the acts of our Assembly, and certain parts of the common law. Then elected Governor. Next, to

---

[1] Jefferson Papers #4128 (1800.)

the Legislature, and to Congress again. Sent to Europe as Minister Plenipotentiary. Appointed Secretary of State to the new Government. Elected Vice-President, and President. And lastly, a Visitor and Rector of the University [of Virginia].

In these different offices, with scarcely any interval between them, I have been in the public service now sixty-one years; and during the far greater part of the time, in foreign countries or in other States.

If it were thought worth while to specify any particular services rendered, I would refer to the specification of them made by the [Virginia] Legislature itself in their Farewell Address on my retiring from the Presidency, February, 1809. There is one, however, not therein specified the most important in its consequences, of any transaction in any portion of my life; to wit, the head I personally made against the federal principles and proceedings during the Administration of Mr. Adams. Their usurpations and violations of the Constitution at that period, and their majority in both Houses of Congress, were so great, so decided, and so daring, that after combating their aggressions, inch by inch, without being able in the least to check their career, the republican leaders thought it would be best for them to give up their useless efforts there, go home, get into their respective Legislatures, embody whatever of resistance they could be formed into, and if ineffectual, to perish there as in the last ditch. All, therefore, retired leaving Mr. Gallatin alone in the House of Representatives, and myself in the Senate, where I then presided as Vice-President.

Remaining at our posts, and bidding defiance to the brow beatings and insults by which they endeavored to drive us off also, we kept the mass of republicans in phalanx together, until the Legislature could be brought up to the charge; and nothing on earth is more certain, than that if myself particularly, placed by my office of Vice-President at the head of the republicans, had given way and withdrawn from my post, the republicans throughout the Union would have given up in despair, and the cause would have been lost forever.

By holding on, we obtained time for the Legislature to come up with their weight; and those of Virginia and Kentucky particularly, but more especially the former, by their celebrated resolutions, saved the Constitution at its last gasp. No person who was not a witness of the scenes of that gloomy period, can form any idea of the afflicting persecutions and personal indignities we had to brook. They saved our country, however. The spirits of the people were so much subdued and reduced to despair by the X. Y. Z. imposture, and other stratagems and machinations, that they would have sunk into apathy and monarchy, as the only form of government which could maintain itself.

If Legislative services are worth mentioning, and the stamp of liberality and equality, which was necessary to be imposed on our laws in the first crisis of our birth as a nation, was of any value, they will find that the leading and most important laws of that day were prepared by myself, and carried chiefly by my

*efforts; supported, indeed, by able and faithful coad-
jutors from the ranks of the house, very effective as
seconds, but who would not have taken the field as
leaders.*

*The prohibition of the further importation of slaves
was the first of these measures in time. This was followed by the abolition of entails, which broke up the
hereditary and high-handed aristocracy, which, by
accumulating immense masses of property in single
lines of families, had divided our country into two
distinct orders, of nobles and plebeians.*

*But further to complete the equality among our citi-
zens so essential to the maintenance of republican
government, it was necessary to abolish the principle
of primogeniture. I drew the law of descents, giving
equal inheritance to sons and daughters, which made
a part of the Revised Code.*

*The attack on the establishment of a dominant reli-
gion was first made by myself. It could be carried at
first only by a suspension of salaries for one year, by
battling it again at the next session for another year,
and so from year to year, until the public mind was
ripened for the bill for establishing religious freedom,
which I had prepared for the Revised Code also. This
was at length established permanently, and by the
efforts chiefly of Mr. Madison, being myself in Europe
at the time that work was brought forward.*

*To these particular services, I think I might add the
establishment of our University, as principally my
work, acknowledging at the same time, as I do, the*

great assistance received from my able colleagues of the Visitation. But my residence in the vicinity threw, of course, on me the chief burthen of the enterprise, as well of the buildings as of the general organization and care of the whole. The effect of this institution on the future fame, fortune and prosperity of our country, can as yet be seen but at a distance. But an hundred well-educated youth, which it will turn out annually, and ere long, will fill all its offices with men of superior qualifications, and raise it from its humble state to an eminence among its associates which it has never yet known; no, not in its brightest days. That institution is now qualified to raise its youth to an order of science unequalled in any other State; and this superiority will be the greater from the free range of mind encouraged there, and the restraint imposed at other seminaries by the shackles of a domineering hierarchy, and a bigoted adhesion to ancient habits. Those now on the theatre of affairs will enjoy the ineffable happiness of seeing themselves succeeded by sons of a grade of science beyond their own ken.[2]

Would you agree to live your life over again if you had the opportunity?

You ask, if I would agree to live my seventy or rather seventy-three years over again? To which I say, yea. I think with you, that it is a good world on the whole; that it has been framed on a principle of benevolence,

---

[2] Thoughts on Lotteries #4129 (M., 1826.)

and more pleasure than pain dealt out to us. There are, indeed, (who might say nay) gloomy and hypo-chondriac minds, inhabitants of diseased bodies, disgusted with the present, and despairing of the future; always counting that the worst will happen, because it may happen. To these I say, how much pain have cost us the evils which have never hap-pened! My temperament is sanguine. I steer my bark with Hope in the head, leaving Fear in the stern. My hopes, indeed, sometimes fail; but not oftener than the forebodings of the gloomy. There are, I acknowledge, even in the happiest life, some terrible convulsions, heavy set-offs against the opposite page of the account.[3]

You had a long, fruitful life, living to the age of eighty-three during a time when the average life expectancy was about thirty seven years of age. Although you lived better than many during your age, it was primitive compared to most those living in the United States today. Tell us of your habits? What did you do to have such a long life?

My health has been always so uniformly firm, that I have for some years dreaded nothing so much as the living too long. I think, however, that a flaw has appeared which ensures me against that, without cutting short any of the period during which I could expect to remain capable of being useful. It will prob-ably give me as many years as I wish, and without pain or debility. Should this be the case, my most anx-ious prayers will have been fulfilled by Heaven. * * *

---

[3] To John Adams #4758   (M., April 1816.)

My florid health is calculated to keep my friends as well as foes quiet, as they should be.[4]

The request of the history of my physical habits would have puzzled me not a little, had it not been for the model with which you accompanied it, of Doctor Rush's answer to a similar inquiry. I live so much like other people, that I might refer to ordinary life as the history of my own. * * * I have lived temperately, eating little animal food, and that not as an aliment, so much as a condiment for the vegetables which constitute my principal diet.

I double, however, the Doctor's glass and a half of wine, and even treble it with a friend; but halve its effects by drinking the weak wines only. The ardent wines I cannot drink, nor do I use ardent spirits in any form. Malt liquors and cider are my table drinks, and my breakfast is of tea and coffee.

I have been blest with organs of digestion which accept and concoct, without ever murmuring, whatever the palate chooses to consign to them, and I have not yet lost a tooth by age. I was a hard student until I entered on the business of life, the duties of which leave no idle time to those disposed to fulfil them; and now, retired, and at the age of seventy-six, I am again a hard student.

Indeed, my fondness for reading and study revolts me from the drudgery of letter writing. And a stiff wrist, the consequence of an early dislocation, makes writing

---

[4] To Dr. Benjamin Rush #4756 (W., 1801.)

both slow and painful. I am not so regular in my sleep as the Doctor says he was, devoting to it from five to eight hours, according as my company or the book I am reading interests me; and I never go to bed without an hour, or half hour s previous reading of something moral, whereon to ruminate in the intervals of sleep. But whether I retire to bed early or late, I rise with the sun. I use spectacles at night, but not necessarily in the day, unless in reading small print. My hearing is distinct in particular conversation, but confused when several voices cross each other, which unfits me for the society of the table. I have been more fortunate than my friend in the article of health. So free from catarrhs that I have not had one (in the breast, I mean) on an average of eight or ten years through life. I ascribe this exemption partly to the habit of bathing my feet in cold water every morning, for sixty years past. A fever of more than twenty-four hours I have not had above two or three times in my life.

A periodical headache has afflicted me occasionally, once, perhaps, in six or eight years, for two or three weeks at a time, which now seems to have left me; and except on a late occasion of indisposition, I enjoy good health; too feeble, indeed, to walk much, but riding without fatigue six or eight miles a day, and sometimes thirty or forty. I may end these egotisms, therefore, as I began, by saying that my life has been so much like that of other people that I might say with Horace, to everyone "nomine mutato, de te fabula narratur" [with the name changed the story applies to you].[5] The Giver of life gave it for happiness

[5] To Doctor Vine Utley #4750 (M., 1819.)

and not for wretchedness.[6]

You lived in a stressful, violent era in our history, with times changing from British rule to the democratic republic founded by you and the other Founding Fathers, many with strong opinions and principles. Would you share with us your principles, those in politics, and those in general life and living?

A part of my occupation, and by no means the least pleasing, is the direction of the studies of such young men as ask it. They place themselves in the neighboring village and have the use of my library and counsel, and make a part of my society. In advising the course of their reading, I endeavor to keep their attention fixed on the main objects of all science, the freedom and happiness of man. So that coming to bear a share in the councils and government of their country, they will keep ever in view the. sole objects of all legitimate government.[7]

In confutation of * * * all future calumnies, by way of anticipation, I shall make to you a profession of my political faith: in confidence that you will consider every future imputation on me of a contrary complexion as bearing on its front the mark of falsity and calumny. I do then, with sincere zeal, wish an inviolable preservation of our Federal Constitution, according to the true sense in which it was adopted by

---

6 To James Monroe #9175 (M., 1782.)
7 To General Kosciusko #9213 (M., 1810.)

the States: that in which it was advocated by its friends, and not that which its enemies apprehended, who therefore became its enemies; and I am opposed to the monarchizing its features by the forms of its administration, with a view to conciliate a first transition to a President and Senate for life, and from that to an hereditary tenure of these offices, and thus to worm out the elective principle.

I am for preserving to the States the powers not yielded by them to the Union, and to the Legislature of the Union its constitutional share in the division of powers; and I am not for transferring all the powers of the States to the General Government, and all those of that Government to the Executive branch.

I am for a government rigorously frugal and simple, applying all the possible savings of the public revenue to the discharge of the national debt; and not for a multiplication of officers and salaries merely to make partizans, and for increasing, by every device, the public debt, on the principle of its being a public blessing.

I am for relying for internal defence on our militia solely, till actual invasion, and for such a naval force only as may protect our coasts and harbors from such depredations as we have experienced; and not for a standing army in time of peace, which may overawe the public sentiment; nor for a navy, which, by its own expenses and the eternal wars in which it will implicate us, will grind us with public burdens and sink us under them.

I am for free commerce with all nations; political connection with none; and little or no diplomatic establishment. And I am not for linking ourselves by new treaties with the quarrels of Europe; entering that field of slaughter to preserve their balance, or joining in the confederacy of kings to war against the principles of liberty.

I am for freedom of religion, and against all manoeuvres to bring about a legal ascendency of one sect over another; for freedom of the press, and against all violations of the Constitution to silence by force and not by reason the complaints or criticisms, just or unjust, of our citizens against the conduct of their agents.

And I am for encouraging the progress of science in all its branches; and not for raising a hue and cry against the sacred name of philosophy; for awing the human mind by stories of raw-head and bloody bones to a distrust of its own vision, and to repose implicitly on that of others; to go backwards instead of forwards to look for improvement; to believe that government, religion, morality, and every other science were in the highest perfection in the ages of the darkest ignorance, and that nothing can ever be devised more perfect than what was established by our forefathers.

To these I will add, that I was a sincere well-wisher to the success of the French Revolution, and still wish it may end in the establishment of a free and well ordered republic; but I have not been insensible under the atrocious depredations they have committed on our commerce. The first object of my heart is my country. In that is embarked my family, my fortune, and my own existence. I have not one farthing of

interest, nor one fibre of attachment out of it, nor a
single motive of preference of any one nation to another, but in proportion as they are more or less
friendly to us.

Whenever you are to do a thing, though it can never
be known but to yourself, ask yourself how you would
act were all the world looking at you, and act accordingly.[8] Of the public transactions in which I have
borne a part, I have kept no narrative with a view of
history. A life of constant action leaves no time for
recording. Always thinking of what is next to be
done, what has been done is dismissed, and soon obliterated from the memory.[9]

I never submitted the whole system of my opinions to
the creed of any party of men whatever, in religion,
in philosophy, in politics, or in anything else, where I
was capable of thinking for myself. Such an addiction
is the last degradation of a free and moral agent. If I
could not go to heaven but with a party, I would not
go there at all.[10]

* * * These are my principles. They are unquestionably
the principles of the great body of our fellow-citizens.[11]

---

[8] To Peter Carr. #54 (Ps., 1785.)
[9] To Mr. Spafford #4100 (M., 1819.)
[10] To Francis Hopkinson #6232 (P., 1789.)
[11] To Elbridge Gerry # 6962 (Pa., January 1799.)

CHRONOLOGY OF THOMAS JEFFERSON

Born at Shadwell, Albemarle Co., Va.	April 2 (O. S.), 13 (N. S.), 1743
Death of his Father, Peter Jefferson	August 17, 1757
Entered William and Mary College	March, 1760
Graduation	April 25, 1762
Entered Law Office of George Wythe	April, 1762
Admitted to Bar	1767
Elected to Virginia House of Burgesses	March, 1769
Marriage to Martha Wayles Skelton	January, 1772
Birth of his First Daughter, Martha	September 27, 1772
Appointed Surveyor of Albemarle County	October, 1773
Birth of Second Daughter, Jane Randolph	April 3, 1774
Elected Deputy to Continental Congress	March, 1775
Attends Continental Congress	June 21, 1775
Death of his Mother	March 31, 1776
Appointed on Committee to prepare Declaration of Independence	June 11, 1776
Draft of Declaration Reported	June 28, 1776
Elected Commissioner to France	September 26, 1776
Attends Virginia Assembly	October, 1776
Appointed on Committee to Revise Virginia Laws	November 6, 1776
Birth of Son	May 28, 1777
Death of Son	June 14, 1777
Birth of Third Daughter, Mary	August 1, 1778
Elected Governor of Virginia	June 1, 1779
Reelected Governor of Virginia	June 1, 1780
Fourth Daughter Born	November 3, 1780
Resigns Governorship	June 1, 1781
Appointed Peace Commissioner by Continental Congress	June 14, 1781
Appointment Declined	June 30, 1781
Attends Virginia Assembly	November 5, 1781
Committee Appointed to State Charges Against Him	November 26, 1781
Elected Delegate to Congress	November 30, 1781
Voted Thanks of Assembly	December 12, 1781
Daughter Lucy Elizabeth Born	May 8, 1782
Death of Mrs. Jefferson	September 6, 1782
Appointed Peace Commissioner to Europe	November 12, 1782
Appointment Withdrawn	April 1, 1783
Elected Delegate to Congress	June 6, 1783
Elected Chairman of Congress	March 12, 1784
Elected Minister to France	May 7, 1784
Arrived in Paris	August 6, 1784
Elected French Minister by Congress	March 10, 1785
Audience at French Court	May 17, 1785
Death of Youngest Daughter, Lucy	November, 1785
Presented to George III. at Windsor	March 22, 1786

That every man shall be made virtuous, by any process whatever, is, indeed, no more to be expected, than that every tree shall be made to bear fruit, and every plant nourishment. The brier and bramble can never become the vine and olive; but their asperities may be softened by culture, and their properties improved to usefulness in the order and economy of the world. And I do hope that, in the present spirit of extending to the great mass of mankind the blessings of instruction, I see a prospect of great advancement in the happiness of the human race; and that this may proceed to an indefinite, although not to an infinite degree.

Jefferson, In Brief

The first object of my heart is my country. In that is embarked my family, my fortune, and my own existence. I have not one farthing of interest, nor one fibre of attachment out of it, nor a single motive of preference of any one nation to another, but in proportion as they are more or less friendly to us.[12] I like the dreams of the future better than the history of the past.[13]

Mr. Jefferson, throughout history people have looked back to rediscover the thoughts and words of great men who have put their life down in writing for others to share in their knowledge.

Selections from my letters, after my death, may come

---

[12] To Elbridge Gerry #6461 (Pa., 1799.)
[13] To John Adams #3334 (M., 1816.)

1

out successively as the maturity of circumstances may render their appearance seasonable.[14]

We, today, some two hundred and twenty five years later desire to gain some of your insight. May we use excerpts of your letters to help inform the citizenry of the way things ought to be?

I know my own principles to be pure, and therefore am not ashamed of them. On the contrary, I wish them known, and therefore willingly express them to every one. They are the same I have acted on from the year 1775 to this day, and are the same, I am sure, with those of the great body of the American people. I only wish the real principles of those who censure mine were also known.[15]

In doing the research for this book, there are roughly 27,000 original documents of yours at the Library of Congress, so you are well documented. However. I have found so many quotes on the internet that are attributable to you but were not said by you.

So many persons have of late found an interest or a passion gratified by imputing to me sayings and writings which I never said or wrote, or by endeavoring to draw me into newspapers to harass me personally, that I have found it necessary for my quiet and my other pursuits to leave them in full possession of the field, and not to take the trouble of contradicting

---

14 To William Johnson #4102 (M., 1823.)
15 To Samuel Smith #6958 (M., 1798.)

them even in private conversation.[16] Every word which goes from me, whether verbally or in writing, becomes the subject of so much malignant distortion, and perverted construction, that I am obliged to caution my friends against admitting the possibility of my letters getting into the public papers or a copy of them to be taken under any degree of confidence.[17]

Well, I am aware that monticello.org does list some of the commonly misattributed quotes to you. It is a site owned by the Thomas Jefferson Foundation, Inc., which preserves your home, Monticello, and your memory. Nearly a half a million people visit your mountaintop each year. Forgive me, I digress.

As to myself, I shall take no part in any discussions. I leave others to judge of what I have done, and to give me exactly the place which they shall think I have occupied. Marshall [Supreme Court Justice] has written libels on one side; others, I suppose, will be written on the other side; and the world will sift both and separate the truth as well as they can.[18]

You had a polygraph to write a copy as you wrote starting in 1804. Did you record all of your actions or did you have secrets? I am sorry to ask, but there are those who expect it of me.

No apologies for writing or speaking to me freely are necessary. On the contrary, nothing my friends can do is so dear to me, and proves to me their friendship so clearly, as the information they give me of their

---

[16] To Alexander White #1775 (M., 1797.)
[17] To Edward Dowse #4627 (W., 1803.)
[18] To John Adams #1776 (M., 1813.)

sentiments and those of others on interesting points where I am to act, and where information and warning are so essential to excite in me that due reflection which ought to precede action.[19]

Essentially, many of the issues we have today in the United States, the United States had when you were a political leader.

Nothing is so desirable to me, as that after mankind shall have been abused by such gross falsehoods as to events while passing, their minds should at length be set to rights by genuine truth. And I can conscientiously declare that as to myself, I wish that not only no act but no thought of mine should be unknown.[20]

Your epitaph written by you tells us what you think was memorable in your life. The original obelisk was donated to the University of Missouri and sits on the Francis Quadrangle.

HERE WAS BURIED
THOMAS JEFFERSON
AUTHOR
OF THE DECLARATION OF
AMERICAN INDEPENDENCE,
OF
THE STATUTE OF VIRGINIA
FOR RELIGIOUS FREEDOM, AND
FATHER OF THE UNIVERSITY
OF VIRGINIA.
BORN APRIL 2d
1743. O. S.
DIED[21] [July 4, 1826]

19 To Wilson C. Nicholas #160 (M., 1803.)
20 To James Main #4098 (W., 1808.)
21 Epitaph of Jefferson #2711

We would like to learn what you have to think about the issues of today as well as those of your day, Later we can talk of more specificities of your philosophy of life.

I shall often go wrong, through defect of judgment. When right, I shall often be thought wrong by those whose positions will not command a view of the whole ground. I ask your indulgence for my own errors, which will never be intentional; and your support against the errors of others, who may condemn what they would not if seen in all its parts.[22]

---

[22] First Inaugural Address #2735 (1801.)

VIEWS ON GOVERNMENT

Our lot has been cast by the favor of heaven in a country and under circumstances highly auspicious to our peace and prosperity, and where no pretence can arise for the degrading and oppressive establishments of Europe. It is our happiness that honorable distinctions flow only from public approbation; and that finds no object in titled dignitaries and pageants. Let us, then, endeavor carefully to guard this happy state of things, by keeping a watchful eye over the disaffection of wealth and ambition to the republican principles of our Constitution, and by sacrificing all our local and personal interests to the cultivation of the Union, and maintenance of the authority of the laws.[23]

How did we end up with a representative government?

---

[23] To Pennsylvania Democratic Republicans #8661 (1809.)

The full experiment of a government democratical, but representative, was and is still reserved for us. The idea (taken, indeed, from the little specimen formerly existing in the English constitution, but now lost) has been carried by us, more or less, into all our legislative and executive departments; but it has not yet, by any of us, been pushed into all the ramifications of the system, so far as to leave no authority existing not responsible to the people; whose rights, however, to the exercise and fruits of their own industry, can never be protected against the selfishness of rulers not subject to their control at short periods.

The introduction of this new principle of representative democracy has rendered useless almost everything written before on the structure of government; and, in a great measure, relieves our regret, if the political writings of Aristotle, or of any other ancient, have been lost, or are unfaithfully rendered or explained to us.[24]

We went through a Revolution and other similar forms of government, before our Constitution and present form of government was founded. As we now start to prepare for the 250th Anniversary of the Declaration of Independence, I ask you, when did the Revolution begin? Was it the Stamp Act? The Boston Tea Party? The Halifax Resolves?

*It would * * * be as difficult to say at what moment the Revolution began, and what incident set it in mo-*

---

[24] To Isaac H. Tiffany #7270 (M., 1816.)

7

tion, as to fix the moment that the embryo becomes an animal, or the act which gives him a beginning.[25]

One of my favorite organizations, the National Society Sons of the American Revolution, is now preparing for the celebration, and have started with the Stamp Act, and are encouraging all Americans to join in the remembrance of our nation's founding. The Bicentennial was important to America as this will be.

The memory of the American Revolution will be immortal, and will immortalize those who record it. The reward is encouraging, and will justify all those pains which a rigorous investigation of facts will render necessary.[26]

Mr. Jefferson, I write this book to inform the citizenry of some of your knowledge and concerns on the government and life in general. Many of the concerns of your day, continue to be the concerns of ours.

The liberty of speaking and writing guards our other liberties.[27] *There are rights which it is useless to surrender to the government, and which governments have yet always been found to invade. [Among] these are the rights of thinking, and publishing our thoughts by speaking or writing.*[28]

For promoting the public happiness, those persons whom nature has endowed with genius and virtue,

25 To John Adams #7474 (M., 1818.)
26 To Hilliard D'Auberteuil #7488 (P., 1786.)
27 Reply to Address #3234 (1808.)
28 To David Humphreys #3233 (P.,1789.)

should be rendered by liberal education worthy to receive, and able to guard the sacred deposit of the rights and liberties of their fellow citizens; and they should be called to that charge without regard to wealth, birth, or other accidental condition or circumstance.[29]

Taking a look at the political climate in the United States today, what do you think the citizenry should do to get the government under control?

I hold that a little rebellion, now and then, is a good thing, and as necessary in the political world as storms are in the physical.[30]

Are you sure you would propose rebellion among the people?

The spirit of resistance to government is so valuable on certain occasions, that I wish it to be always kept alive. It will often be exercised when wrong, but better so than not to be exercised at all.[31]

Mr. Jefferson, rebellions are understandable in the wild and new times in which you lived, but in modern orderly days?

What country can preserve its liberties if its rulers are not warned, from time to time, that the people preserve the spirit of resistance? Let them take arms. The remedy is to set them right as to facts, pardon and pacify them.[32]

---

[29]Diffusion of Knowledge Bill #3435 (1779.)
[30] To James Madison #7172 (P., 1787.)
[31] To Mrs. John Adams #7174 (P., 1787.)
[32] To W. S. Smith #4175 (P., 1787.)

The people seem to be the power in the governments set up by the Constitution. Do you think that it is sometimes necessary to remind our elected officials that they are employed by the voters, that they are in office to insure our rights and safety?

The constitutions of most of our States assert, that all power is inherent in the people; that they may exercise it by themselves, in all cases to which they think themselves competent, (as in electing their functionaries executive and legislative, and deciding by a jury of themselves, both fact and law, in all judiciary cases in which any fact is involved) or they may act by representatives, freely and equally chosen;

You may not know this, but the federal and state governments are limiting our rights in regard to the ownership, carrying and use of weapons.

That it is their right and duty to be at all times armed; that they are entitled to freedom of person, freedom of religion, freedom of property, and freedom of the press.[33]

What if the rebellion is unsuccessful?

Unsuccessful rebellions generally establish the encroachments on the rights of people which have produced them. An Observation of this truth should render honest republican governors so mild in their punishment of rebellions, as not to discourage them too much.[34]

---

[33] To John Cartwright, LOC (M., June 5, 1824)
   http://hdl.loc.gov/loc.mss/mtj.mtjbib025031
[34] To James Madison #7176 (P., 1787.)

Mr. Jefferson, you sound like a radical revolutionary!

I like a little rebellion now and then. It is like a storm in the atmosphere.[35]

Really, now isn't an armed rebellion a means of last resort. With violence, when your dead your dead. Wouldn't it make more since to have a rebellion of minds, wits and the ballot box.

Everyone must act according to the dictates of his own reason.[36] *Possessed of the blessing of and self-government, of such a portion of civil liberty as no other civilized nation enjoys, it now behooves us to guard and preserve them by a continuance of the sacrifices and exertions by which they were acquired, and especially to nourish that Union which is their sole guarantee.*[37]

My lovely wife, asked, "what is the purpose of our conversation today?"

I am very much in hopes we shall be able to restore union to our country. Not, indeed, that the Federal leaders can be brought over. They are invincibles; but I really hope their followers may. The bulk of these were real republicans...[38]

Your definition of republican is different than the Republican Party.

---

[35] To Mrs. John Adams #7177 (P. 1787.)
[36] To Rev. Samuel Miller #7157 (W., 1808.)
[37] To New London Plymouth Society #8672 (1809.)
[38] To John Paige #135 (W., 1801.)

* * * *men, enjoying in ease and security the full fruits of their own industry, enlisted by all their interests on the side of law and order, habituated to think for themselves, and to follow their reason as their guide, would be more easily and safely governed than with minds nourished in error, and vitiated and debased, as in Europe, by ignorance, indigence and oppression.[39]*

The people through all the States are for republican forms, republican principles, simplicity, economy, religious and civil freedom.[40]

In the United States today, do you think we have a chance at changing our current system of government to the way it was set up under the constitution?

My theory has always been, that if we are to dream, the flatteries of hope are as cheap, and pleasanter than the gloom of despair.[41] Unequivocal in principle, reasonable in manner, we shall be able, I hope, to do a great deal of good to the cause of freedom and harmony.[42]

Isn't it difficult for men to run the country as it was framed in the constitution?

The ordinary affairs of a nation offer little difficulty to a person of any experience.[43] There are no mysteries in the public administration. Difficulties indeed

---

[39] To William Johnson #3945 (M., 1823.)
[40] To E. Livingston #7345 (Pa., 1800.)
[41] To M. de Marbois #3795 (M., 1817.)
[42] To Elbridge Gerry #137 (W., 1801.)
[43] To James Sullivan #139 (W., 1808.)

sometimes arise; but common sense and honest intentions will generally steer through them, and, where they cannot be surmounted, I have ever seen the well intentioned part of our fellow citizens sufficiently disposed not to look for impossibilities.[44]

Many individuals believe that a lack of character is the problem with many of our current officeholders including the President and his appointees. Look at what we are currently enduring.

I sincerely wish we could see our government so secured as to depend less on the character of the person in whose hands it is trusted.

President Obama endorsed Hillary Clinton, of the Democrat Party, who had an FBI investigation going on for providing "materially false" information to the FBI and mishandling classified information as the Secretary of State, a position which you were first to hold. The FBI Director Comey said she was super bad but not gross when she neglected our Nation's secret. He said it wasn't intentional, that she may not have known the law, and let her off.

Man once surrendering his reason, has no remaining guard against absurdities the most monstrous, and like a ship without rudder, is the sport of every wind.[45] *Laws will be * * * honestly administered, in proportion as those who * * * administer them are wise and honest.*[46]

---

44 To Dr. J. B. Stuart #132 (M., 1817.)
45 To James Smith #7164 (M., 1822.)
46 Diffusion of Knowledge Bill #4477 (1779.)

She gets off without even a hand slap where others would not.

The public say from all quarters that they wish to hear reason and not disgusting blackguardism.[47] Ignorance of the law is no excuse in any country. If it were, the laws would lose their effect, because it can be always pretended.[48] An equal application of law to every condition of man is fundamental.[49] Bad men will sometimes get in, and make great progress in corrupting the public mind and principles. This is a subject with which wisdom and patriotism should be occupied.[50]

Can you name one difference between you and Hillary Clinton?

Opinion is power.[51] I readily suppose my opinion wrong, when opposed by the majority.[52] Public opinion is a censor before which the most exalted tremble for their future as well as present fame.[53]

Any advice for Hillary Clinton and anyone else in hot water?

If you ever find yourself environed with difficulties and perplexing circumstances, out of which you are at a loss how to extricate yourself, do what is right, and be assured that that will extricate you the best out of the worst situations. Though you cannot see,

[47] To James Madison #7163 (Pa., 1799.)
[48] To M. Limozin #4505 (P., 1787.)
[49] To George Hay #4493 (M., 1807.)
[50] To Moses Robinson #6897 (W., 1801.)
[51] To John Adams #6235 (M., 1816.)
[52] To James Madison #6234 (P., 1788.)
[53] To John Adams #6246 (M., 1816.)

when you take one step, what will be the next, yet fol-
low truth, justice, and plain dealing, and never fear
their leading you out of the labyrinth, in the easiest
manner possible. The knot which you thought a
Gordian one, will untie itself before you. Nothing is so
mistaken as the supposition that a person is to extri-
cate himself from a difficulty by intrigue, by chican-
ery, by dissimulation, by trimming, by an untruth, by
an injustice. This increases the difficulties tenfold;
and those, who pursue these methods, get themselves
so involved at length, that they can turn no way but
their infamy becomes more exposed.[54] He who knows
nothing is nearer the truth than he whose mind is
filled with falsehoods and errors.[55]

When we have elections and political appointments, should
the actions of these individuals be looked at? So often any-
more, we find candidates and appointees lacking in what
many Americans desire.

The uniform tenor of a man's life furnishes better ev-
idence of what he has said or done on any particular
occasion than the word of any enemy, and of an ene-
my, too, who shows that he prefers the use of false-
hoods which suit him to truths which do not.[56] I think
it a duty in those intrusted with the administration
of their affairs to conform themselves to the decided
choice of their constituents.[57]

---

[54] To Peter Carr #2223 (P., 1785.)
[55] To John Norvell #2863 (W., 1807.)
[56] To De Witt Clinton #1190 (W., 1803.)
[57] To John Jay #6249 (P., 1785.)

Common sense and morality is the problem nowadays. Morality and honesty are not taught to many children. Parents are busy trying to get ahead in the world and the public schools, they think morality is a religion and should not be taught.

*I believe * * * that the moral sense is as much a part of our constitution as that of feeling, seeing, or hearing;* [58]

Do you think that some people of high character are put into public service and encouraged to stay?

There is sometimes an eminence of character on which society have such peculiar claims as to control the predilections of the individual for a particular walk of happiness, and restrain him to that alone arise.

What do you think of the recent Congressional elections in which the Republicans took over the control of the Senate and the House of Representatives?

The order and good sense displayed in this recovery from delusion, and in the momentous crisis which lately arose, really bespeak a strength of character in our nation which augurs well for the duration of our Republic; and I am much better satisfied now of its stability than I was before it was tried. [59]

Mr. Jefferson, several states in the Union have passed laws seeking term limits of officeholders. What is your opinion of states enacting term limits for congressional elections?

58 To Jon Adams #5516 (M., 1816.)
59 To Dr. Joseph Priestly #1194 (W., 1801.)

Would a constitutional amendment be required because the Constitution does not exclude re-elections or can the states pass laws to add qualifications?

You ask my opinion on the question, whether the States can add any qualifications to those which the Constitution has pre-scribed for their members of Congress? It is a question I had never before reflected on; yet had taken up an off handed opinion, agreeing with your first, that they could not; that to add new qualifications to those of the Constitution, would be as much an alteration as to detract from them. And so I think the House of Representatives decided in some case; I believe that of a member from Baltimore.

But your letter having induced me to look into the Constitution, and to consider the question a little, I am again in your predicament, of doubting the correctness of my first opinion. Had the Constitution been silent, nobody can doubt but that the right to prescribe all the qualifications of those they would send to represent them, would have belonged to the State. So also the Constitution might have prescribed the whole, and excluded all others.

It seems to have preferred the middle way. It has exercised the power in part, by declaring some dis-qualifications, to wit, those of not being twenty-five years of age, of not having been a citizen seven years, and of not being an inhabitant of the State at the time of election. But it does not declare, itself, that the member shall not be a lunatic, a pauper, a convict of treason, of murder, of felony, or other infamous crime, or a non-resident of his district; nor does it prohibit to the State the power of declaring these, or any other disqualifications which its particular circumstances may call for; and these may be different in different States. Of course, then, by the tenth amendment, the power is reserved for the State.[60]

So it sounds to me like it may be possible for States to enact term limits on Congressmen.

If, wherever the Constitution assumes a single power out of many which belong to the same subject, we should consider it as assuming the whole, it would vest the General Government with a mass of power never contemplated. On the contrary, the assumption of particular powers seems an exclusion of all not assumed. This reasoning appears to me to be sound; but, on so recent a change of view, caution requires us not to be too confident, and that we admit this to be one of the doubtful questions on which honest men may differ with the purest motives; and the more readily, as we find we have differed from ourselves.[61]

That sounds more like an answer from a lawyer instead of a farmer. What do you think, should all those elected to Congress, to make laws, be lawyers?

Their trade is to question everything, yield nothing and talk by the hour. That one hundred and fifty lawyers should do business together ought not to be

---

[60] To Joseph C. Cabell #1577 (M., 1814.)
[61] To Joseph C. Cabell #1577 (M., 1814.)

expected.[62]

Well then, who should be elected?

Congress is the great commanding theatre of this nation, and the threshold to whatever department of office a man is qualified to enter.[63] *We want men of business [in Congress].* * * * *I am convinced it is in the power of any man who understands business, and who will undertake to keep a file of the business before Congress and press it, as he would his own docket in a court, to shorten the sessions a month one year with another, and to save in that way $30,000 a year. An ill-judged modesty prevents those from undertaking it who are equal to it.*[64]

There are oftentimes accusations of Congressmen enriching themselves by legislating to improve the value of their stock holdings. They buy and sell stocks on insider information, legally, while the rest of the American citizens have legal charges brought up against them, as Martha Stewart had. Even the former First Lady, Hillary Clinton has been accused of doing this in stocks of drug companies and in cattle futures. What would you propose to help alleviate the problem?

It [is] a cause of just uneasiness, when we [see] a legislature legislating for their own interests, in opposition to those of the people.[65]

I told President Washington that my wish was to see

---

[62] Autobiography #4554 (1821.)
[63] To William Wirt #1560 (W., 1808.)
[64] To Caesar A. Rodney #1508 (W., 1802)
[65] The Anas #1519 (1792.)

both Houses of Congress cleansed of all persons interested in the bank or public stocks; and that a pure Legislature being given us, I should always be ready to acquiesce under their determinations, even if contrary to my own opinions; for that I subscribe to the principle, that the will of the majority, honestly expressed, should give law.[66]

How can we correct this corruption with our elected officials? The will of the majority was honestly expressed and generally ignored, overruled by the President and Congress concerning insider trading.

The only corrective of what is corrupt in our present form of government will be the augmentation of the members in the lower House so as to get a more agricultural representation, which may put that interest above that of the stockjobbers.[67]

So do you think elections will take care of the problems of Congress?

A jealous care of the right of election by the people, --- a mild and safe corrective of abuses which are lopped by the sword of revolution where peaceable remedies are unprovided, I deem [one of the] essential principles of our government and, consequently, [one] which ought to shape its administration.[68]

It was probably from this view of the encroaching character of privilege, that the framers of our Consti-

---

[66] The Anas #1593 (Feb. 1793.)
[67] To George Mason #1533 (PA., 1791.)
[68] First Inaugural Address #2428 (1801.)

tution, in their care to provide that the laws shall bind equally on all, and especially that those who make them shall not be exempt themselves from their operation, have only privileged "Senators and Representatives" themselves from the single act of arrest in all cases except treason, felony, and breach of the peace, during their attendance at the session of their respective Houses, and in going to and returning from the same, and from being questioned in any other place for any speech or debate in either House.[69]

You did that in the election of 1800, You called it the second Revolution.

The revolution of 1800 was as real a revolution in the principles of our government as that of 1776 was in its form; not effected, indeed, by the sword, as that, but by the rational and peaceable instrument of reform, the suffrage of the people.[70]

I was only of a band devoted to the cause of Independence, all of whom exerted equally their best endeavors for its success, and have a common right to the merits of its acquisition. So also is the civil revolution of 1801. Very many and very meritorious were the worthy patriots who assisted in bringing back our government to its republican tack.[71]

Unfortunately, the elections in the United States do not have a jealous care. Some of us are looking for the Revolution of

---

[69] Parliamentary Manual #1574
[70] To Spencer Roane #7205 (P.F., 1819.)
[71] To William T. Barry #7836 (M., 1822.)

2016. It is getting to a place where people vote based on what the government will give them. We have had Congressmen, who have broken laws, get reelected. We have candidates who are under criminal investigations get the vote of the people.

[We] should look forward to a time, and that not a distant one, when a corruption in this, as in the country from which we derive our origin, will have seized the heads of government, and be spread by them through the body of the people; when they will purchase the voices of the people, and make them pay the price. Human nature is the same on every side of the Atlantic, and will be alike influenced by the same causes.[72]
But it is said that people vote their pocketbook, what can "I" get, or "how will it help my business."

It is rare that the public sentiment decides immorally or unwisely, and the individual who differs from it ought to distrust and examine well his own opinion.[73]

I believe that the Republicans have a great chance in turning things around. In the words of a great Republican, President Abraham Lincoln, "that this nation, under God, shall have a new birth of freedom - and that government of the people, by the people, for the people, shall not perish from the earth."

To take from one, because it is thought that his own industry and that of his father has acquired too much, in order to spare to others, who, or whose fathers have not exercised equal industry and skill, is

---

[72] Notes on Virginia #1834 (1782.)
[73] To William Findley #6266 (W., March 1801.)

to violate arbitrarily the first principle of association, the <u>guarantee</u> to every one of a free exercise of his industry, & the fruits acquired by it.[74]

Oh my, Mr. Jefferson, If you only knew what restrictions are placed on businesses.

We are to guard against ourselves; not against ourselves as we are, but as we may be; for who can now imagine what we may become under circumstances not now imaginable?[75]

*In questions of power * * * let no more be heard of confidence in man, but bind him down from mischief by the chains of the Constitution.*[76]

Whenever the General Government assumes undelegated powers, its acts are unauthoritative, void, and of no force.[77]

The Government has learned to extort monies from businesses now. Instead of sending corporate crooks to jail, they fine the companies millions and billions of dollars for wrong doing. No one goes to jail, and the wrong doings and the supposed wrong doings of businesses continue.

Every government degenerates when trusted to the rulers of the people alone. The people themselves, therefore, are its only safe depositories. And to render

---

[74] To Joseph Milligan, LOC (M., April 6, 1816.)
   http://hdl.loc.gov/loc.mss/mtj.mtjbib022403
[75] To Jedediah Morse #13 (M., 1822.)
[76] Kentucky Resolutions #7094 (1798.)
[77] Kentucky Resolutions #6852 (1798.)

even them safe, their minds must be improved to a certain degree.[78]

Well it costs the stockholders. Those in corporate business figure it is better to be fined the millions and billions to make even more. It needs to stop.

My confidence is that there will for a long time be virtue and good sense enough in our countrymen to correct abuses.[79] *Private fortunes are destroyed by public as well as by private extravagance.*[80]

We mentioned elections here, so let us step into the subject of political parties. I know earlier, you mentioning not following or prescribing every belief of or to a party. Please tell us more.

Men by their constitutions are naturally divided into two parties:

1. *Those who fear and distrust the people, and wish to draw all powers from them into the hands of the higher classes.*

2. *Those who identify themselves with the people, have confidence in them, cherish and consider them as the most honest and safe, although not the most wise depositary of the public interests.*

In every country these two parties exist, and in every one where they are free to think, speak and write,

---

[78] Notes on Virginia #3534 (1782.)
[79] To E. Rutledge #16 (P., 1788.)
[80] To Samuel Kerchival #2848 (M., 1816.)

*they will declare themselves. Call them, therefore, lib-
erals and serviles, Jacobins and ultras, whigs and
tories, republicans and federalists, aristocrats and
democrats, or by whatever name you please, they are
the same parties still, and pursue the same object. The
last appellation of aristocrats and democrats is the
true one expressing the essence of all.*[81]

We have two main parties now, Republicans and Democrats.
It seems their beliefs change back and forth over the years.
There is the Tea Party, a splinter group with a large following
has come about to try to get the country and the Constitution
back to the people.

*In every free and deliberating society, there must,
from the nature of man, be opposite parties, and
violent dissensions and discords; and one of these, for
the most part, must prevail over the other for a longer or shorter time.*[82] *The greatest good we can do our
country is to heal its party divisions, and make them
one people.*[83]

We have a strong split in our country now. The citizens, I
believe, are thinking there is not much difference between the
two parties and have gone for a candidate, a businessman,
who has not been in the game of politics before. What is
interesting is, some of the Republican candidates, who signed
an agreement to support the primary winner, have said that
they might support the Democrat, Hillary Clinton, the one
under investigation. Now is that a messed up scenario?

[81] To H. Lee #6431 (M., 1824.)
[82] To John Taylor #6433 (Pa., 1798.)
[83] To John Dickinson #3675 (W., July 1801.)

*Both of our political parties, at least the honest part
of them, agree conscientiously in the same object - the
public good; but they differ essentially in what they
deem the means of promoting that good. One side believes it best done by one composition of the governing powers; the other, by a different one. One fears
most the ignorance of the people; the other, the selfishness of rulers independent of them. Which is right,
time and experience will prove. We think that one
side of this experiment has been long enough tried,
and proved not to promote the good of the many; and
that the other has not been fairly and sufficiently
tried. Our opponents think the reverse. With whichever opinion the body of the nation concurs, that
must prevail.*[84]

It is amazing to see what has happened in the parties. The
Republicans were the ones to finally free the slaves, to give
the Blacks a right to vote in the 1860's and to support the
civil rights of the 1960's, but the Democrats, who have made
the Blacks and the poor a slave to their welfare state, has
brought them to their voting camp. Unfortunately, the Democrat's welfare plan also benefits the splitting up of families
so they can get more funds from the government.

*There is an enemy somewhere endeavoring to sow
discord among us. Instead of listening first, then
doubting, and lastly believing anile tales handed
round without an atom of evidence, if my friends will
address themselves to me directly, as you have done,
they shall be informed with frankness and thankful-*

[84] To Mrs. John Adams #6442 (M., 1804.)

ness.[85] *The whole art of government consists in the art of being honest.*[86]

We have that serious discord going on now, with the Democrats and the Republicans. A big divider in the country is in regards to Planned Parenthood and other abortion providers. The Democrats, instead of helping the Blacks and minorities, have come up with promoting abortions to kill their babies legally.

Error of opinion may be tolerated where reason is left free to combat it.[87]

States have made laws to make abortion illegal, and the Supreme Court overthrows the state laws. It is the suppression of religious freedom.

There is more honor and magnanimity in correcting than persevering in an error.[88]

If you look at a map of our country, when it is shaded in the red and blue, by counties, as all of us come to know, you find it seems to be divided as a rural/city conflict. What is really interesting is that the Democrat party, that wants strong Federal Government control, claims you as their founder!

It has been so impossible to contradict all their lies, that I have determined to contradict none; for while I should be engaged with one, they would publish twenty

---

[85] To William Duane #4729 (W., 1806.)
[86] Rights of British America #3476 (1774.)
[87] First Inaugural Address #2745 (1801.)
[88] Batture Case #2724 (1812.)

new ones. Thirty years of public life have enabled most of those who read newspapers to judge of one for themselves.[89]

Party animosities here have raised a wall of separation between those who differ in political sentiments. They must love misery indeed who would rather, at the sight of an honest man, feel the torment of hatred and aversion than the benign spasms of benevolence and esteem.[90] That each party endeavors to get into the administration of the government, and exclude the other from power, is true, and may be stated as a motive of action: but this is only secondary; the primary motive being a real and radical difference of political principle. I sincerely wish our differences were but personally who should govern, and that the principles of our Constitution were those of both parties. Unfortunately, it is otherwise; and the question of preference between monarchy and republicanism, which has so long divided mankind elsewhere, threatens a permanent division here.

And to remember that we are Republic, where we elect citizens to represent us within the government, not a democracy.

Composed, as we were, of the landed and laboring interests of the country, we could not be less anxious for a government of law and order than were the inhabitants of the cities, the strongholds of federalism.[91]

89 To James Monroe #4733 (Ep., May 1800.)
90 To Mrs. Church #366 (Pa., Oct. 1792.)
91 To William Johnson, LOC (M., June 12, 1823)
   http://hdl.loc.gov/loc.mss/mtj.mtjbib024682

When they get piled upon one another in large cities, as in Europe, they will become as corrupt as in Europe.[92] *I view great cities as pestilential to the morals, the health, and the liberties of man. True, they nourish some of the elegant arts, but the useful ones can thrive elsewhere, and less perfection in the others, with more health, virtue and freedom, would be my choice.*[93]

Your comments sound a lot like Ted Cruz, a former Republican presidential candidate, who made what some would call disparaging remarks about New York City.

Where a Constitution, like ours, wears a mixed aspect of monarchy and republicanism, its citizens will naturally divide into two classes of sentiment according to their tone of body or mind. Their habits, connections and callings induce them to wish to strengthen either the monarchical or the republican features of the Constitution. Some will consider it as an elective monarchy, which had better be made hereditary, and, therefore, endeavor to lead towards that all the forms and principles of its administration. Others will view it as an energetic republic, turning in all its points on the pivot of free and frequent elections. The great body of our native citizens are unquestionably of the republican sentiment.

---

[92] To James Madison, LOC (P., Dec. 20, 1787.)
    http://hdl.loc.gov/loc.mss/mjm.03_0150_0154
[93] To Dr. Benjamin Rush #1278 (M., 1800.)

Foreign education, and foreign conventions of interest, have produced some exceptions in every part of the Union, North and South, and perhaps other circumstances in your quarter, better known to you, may have thrown into the scale of exceptions a greater number of the rich. Still there, I believe, and here [the South] I am sure, the great mass is republican. Nor do any of the forms in which the public disposition has been pronounced in the last half dozen years, evince the contrary.

All of them, when traced to their true source, have only been evidences of the preponderant popularity of a particular great character. That influence once withdrawn, and our countrymen left to the operation of their own unbiased good sense, I have no doubt we shall see a pretty rapid return of general harmony, and our citizens moving in phalanx in the paths of regular liberty, order, and a sacrosanct adherence to the Constitution.[94]

Let us talk about the constitution, and then follow it up with the three branches of government.

---

[94] To James Sullivan #6443 (M., Feb. 1797.)

ON THE CONSTITUTION

My God! how little do my countrymen know what precious blessings they are in possession of, and which no other people on earth enjoy. [95] *There are not, on the face of the earth, more tranquil governments than ours, nor a happier and more contented people.*[96]

That is true, but revisionist are always trying to rewrite history and the founding of the United States of America.

Every country is divided between the parties of honest men and rogues.[97] *History may distort truth, and will distort it for a time, by the superior efforts at justification of those who are conscious of needing*

---

[95] To James Monroe #3578 (1785.)
[96] To Baron Geismer #3579 (P., 1785.)
[97] To William B. Giles # 3780 (1795)

it most. Nor will the opening scenes of our present government be seen in their true aspect until the letters of the day, now held in private hoards, shall be broken up and laid open to public view.[98]

So here we are Mr. Jefferson, learning your views of the Federal Government and the Constitution. You were a prolific writer and also kept copies, so we have a considerable amount of resources. History has distorted the views on constitutional powers and it seems we are on a spiral decline in the last fifty years.

About to enter, fellow citizens, on the exercise of duties which comprehend everything dear and valuable to you, it is proper that you should understand what I deem the essential principles of our government, and consequently those which ought to shape its administration. I will compress them within the narrowest compass they will bear, stating the general principle, but not all its limitations.

Equal and exact justice to all men, of whatever state or persuasion, religious or political; peace, commerce and honest friendship with all nations, entangling alliances with none; the support of the State governments in all their rights, as the most competent administrations for our domestic concerns, and the surest bulwark against anti-republican tendencies; the preservation of the General Government in its

---

[98] To William Johnson, LOC (M., June 12, 1823.)
http://hdl.loc.gov/loc.mss/mtj.mtjbib024682

whole constitutional vigor, as the sheet anchor of our peace at home and safety abroad; a jealous care of the right of election by the people a mild and safe corrective of abuses, which are lopped by the sword of revolution, where peaceable remedies are unprovided; absolute acquiescence in the decisions of the majority the vital principle of republics, from which there is no appeal but to force, the vital principle and immediate parent of despotism; a well disciplined militia our best reliance in peace and for the first moments of war, till regulars may relieve them; the supremacy of the civil over the military authority; economy in the public expense, that labor may be lightly burdened; the honest payment of our debts and sacred preservation of the public faith; encouragement of agriculture, and of commerce as its handmaid; the diffusion of information, and the arraignment of all abuses at the bar of public reason; freedom of religion; freedom of the press; freedom of person, under the protection of the habeas corpus; and trial by juries impartially selected.

These principles form the bright constellation which has gone before us, and guided our steps through an age of revolution and reformation. The wisdom of our sages and the blood of our heroes have been devoted to their attainment. They should be the creed of our political faith; the text of civil instruction; the touchstone by which to try the services of those we trust; and should we wander from them in moments of error or alarm, let us hasten to retrace our steps, and to regain the road which alone leads to peace, liberty, and safety.[99]

From your very first comment, "equal and exact justice to all men, of whatever state or persuasion," we now find difficulty. We have Hillary Clinton. The FBI found she had mishandled classified materials, with people wanting to do the United States harm, no doubt accessing the documents. She gets off scot free, while others doing less are sitting in prison.

*Mankind soon learns to make interested uses of every right and power which they possess, or may assume. The public money and public liberty * * * will soon be discovered to be sources of wealth and dominion to those who hold them; distinguished, too, by this tempting circumstance, that they are the instrument, as well as the object of acquisition. With money we will get men, said Caesar, and with men we will get money.*[100] *Deal out justice without partiality or favoritism.*[101]

President Obama recently lost a Supreme Court battle regarding his Executive Order regarding shielding of millions of illegal immigrants and make them eligible for work permits without the approval from Congress. It is not fair to the ones coming into the country legally.

Education is the true corrective of abuses of constitutional power.[102]

---

99 First Inaugural Address #2927 (1801.)
100 Notes on Virginia #25 (1792.)
101 To Hugh Williamson #2905 (Pa., 1792.)
102 To William C. Jarvis #18 (M., 1820.)

There are more than 11 million illegal immigrants in the United States according to the government. It seems if you can count them, give them welfare and drivers licenses, you could deport them. Some say there are up to 30 million illegals now. Are you aware, the Truman and Eisenhower Administrations had 5.5 million illegals leave the United States either through deportation or the threat of it?

Our citizens have wisely formed themselves into one nation as to others, and several States as among themselves. To the united nation belong our external and mutual relations; to each State, severally, the care of our persons, our property, our reputation and religious freedom. This wise distribution, if carefully preserved, will prove, I trust from example, that while smaller governments are better adapted to the ordinary objects of society, larger confederations more effectually secure independence, and the preservation of republican government.[103]

In founding our nation, it appears that the Federal Government was to have only a small part in the overall affairs of the citizens, as compared to the States. When you talk of the united nation, you talk of the United States, not the UN and the New World Order. In regards to the Constitution.......

I was in Europe when the Constitution was planned, and never saw it till after it was established. On receiving it, I wrote strongly to Mr. Madison, urging the want of provision for the freedom of religion, freedom of the press, trial by jury, habeas corpus, and

---

[103] To the Rhode Island Assembly #2936 (W., May 1801.)

substitution of militia for a standing army, and an express reservation to the State of all rights not specifically granted to the Union. He accordingly moved in the first session of Congress for these amendments, which were agreed to and ratified by the States as they now stand. This is all the hand I had in what related to the Constitution.[104]

You did provide input on the Bill of Rights. How important the Bill of Rights is to Americans and how the government tries to twist it away from us.

No constitution was ever before so well calculated as ours for extensive empire and self-government.[105] The true theory of our Constitution is surely the wisest and best, that the States are independent as to everything within themselves, and united as to everything respecting foreign affairs. Let the General Government be reduced to foreign concerns only, and let our affairs be disentangled from those of all other nations, except as to commerce, which the merchants will manage the better, the more they are left free to manage for themselves, and our General Government may be reduced to a very simple organization, and a very inexpensive one; a few plain duties to be performed by a few servants.[106]

I wish it was that easy, Mr. Jefferson. You wouldn't recognize it any more. As you can see, we have a large expensive Federal Government where it is involved in all aspects of our lives,

---

[104] To Dr. Joseph Priestly #1689 (W.. 1802.)
[105] To President Madison #1707 (M., April 1809.)
[106] To Gideon Granger #1707 (M., 1800.)

liberties and freedom. The idea of States rights is all but gone from the practical operations of the Federal Government. The concept of a small Federal Government has been lost, and unfortunately the citizens are unaware that the Constitution set it up to be small. The Federal Government does not work for the people, but itself. The people, however, believe that they must rely on the government.

I am for preserving to the States the powers not yielded by them to the Union and to the Legislature of the Union its constitutional share in the division of powers; and I am not for transferring all the powers of the States to the General Government, and all those of that government to the Executive branch.[107]

Unfortunately, Mr. Jefferson, the Federal Government extorts and blackmails the States with funds and resources they have taxed from the citizens. This is done with the roads, with education, and more recently with bathrooms. The national elected officials do it to push their social agenda and the bureaucrats make up rules and regulations to justify their jobs, and to increase their little power base, not for the benefit of the citizens.

I recollect but one instance of control vested in the Federal over the State authorities, in a matter purely domestic, which is that of metallic tenders.[108]

You have seen the practices by which the public servants have been able to cover their conduct, or, where

---

[107] To Elbridge Gerry #8138 (1799.)
[108] To Robert J. Garnett #8135 (M., 1824.)

that could not be done, delusions by which they have varnished it for the eye of their constituents. What an augmentation of the field for jobbing, speculating, plundering, office-building and office hunting would be produced by an assumption of all the State powers into the hands of the General Government.[109]

Well, it is done so much, that the public thinks it is the way it is supposed to be.

Our country is too large to have all its affairs directed by a single government. Public servants at such a distance, and from under the eye of their constituents, must, from the circumstance of distance, be unable to administer and overlook all the details necessary for the good government of the citizens; and the same circumstance, by rendering detection impossible to their constituents, will invite the public agents to corruption, plunder and waste.[110]

It is not by the consolidation, or concentration of powers, but by their distribution, that good government is effected. Were not this great country already divided into States, that division must be made, that each might do for itself what concerns itself directly, and what it can so much better do than a distant authority. Every State again is divided into counties, each to take care of what lies within its local bounds; each county again into townships or wards, to manage minuter details; and every ward into farms, to be

---

[109] To Gideon Granger #1168 (M., Aug. 1800.)
[110] To Gideon Granger #1179 (M., Aug. 1800.)

*governed each by its individual proprietor. * * * It is by this partition of cares, descending in gradation from general to particular, that the mass of human affairs may be best managed, for the good and prosperity of all.*[111]

So you are saying that the government operates best when it is closer to the citizens. What are we to do.

In government, as well as in every other business of life, it is by division and sub-division of duties alone, that all matters, great and small, can be managed to perfection.[112]

The tree of liberty must be refreshed from time to time with the blood of patriots and tyrants. It is its natural manure.[113]

Come now Mr. Jefferson is that how you really feel? You were the third President and I did not see you send out a call to arms during your presidency and even before when the centralization and usurpation of power at the federal level started.

If no action is to be deemed virtuous for which malice can imagine a sinister motive, then there never was a virtuous action; no, not even in the life of our Saviour Himself. But He has taught us to judge the tree by its

---

[111] Autobiography #1176 (1821.)
[112] To Samuel Kerchival #2207 (M., 1816.)
[113] To W. S. Smith #4665 (P., 1787.)

fruit, and to leave motives to Him who can alone see into them.[114]

I have been blamed for saying, that a prevalence of the doctrines of consolidation would one day call for reformation or revolution. I answer by asking if a single State of the Union would have agreed to the Constitution had it given all powers to the General Government? If the whole opposition to it did not proceed from the jealousy and fear of every State, of being subjected to the other States in matters merely its own? And if there is any reason to believe the States more disposed now than then, to acquiesce in this general surrender of all their rights and powers to a consolidated government, one and undivided?[115]

I doubt we would have our country if the States would have known of the power grab of the Federal Government.

I see with the deepest affliction, the rapid strides with which the Federal branch of our government is advancing towards the usurpation of all the rights reserved to the States, and the consolidation in itself of all powers, foreign and domestic; and that too, by constructions which, if legitimate, leave no limits to their power. Take together the decisions of the Federal Court, the doctrines of the President, and the misconstructions of the constitutional compact acted on by the legislature of the Federal branch, and it is but too evident, that the three ruling branches of that

[114] To Martin Van Buren #56 (M., 1824.)
[115] To Samuel Johnson #1182 (M., 1823.)

department are in combination to strip their colleagues, the State authorities, of the powers reserved by them, and to exercise themselves all functions foreign and domestic.

The best example of this was Obamacare. No constitutional basis for the Federal Government to provide healthcare to the people. The President promoted it, Congress passed it and the Supreme court upheld it. Where is it in the Constitution?

Under the power to regulate commerce, they assume indefinitely that also over agriculture and manufactures, and call it regulation to take the earnings of one of these branches of industry, and that, too, the most depressed, and put them into the pockets of the other, the most flourishing of all. Under the authority to establish post roads, they claim that of cutting down mountains for the construction of roads, of digging canals, and aided by a little sophistry on the words "general welfare," a right to do, not only the acts to effect that, which are specifically enumerated and permitted, but whatsoever they shall think, or pretend will be for the general welfare.

So you do not want the Federal Highway Commission? The interstate system was initially justified for the national defense. Now it seems the Federal Government take taxes from the citizens, then it pays back to the states 80% of the cost of the city, county and state roads in a state they want to approve. Like the Federal Government knows best.

And what is our resource for the preservation of the Constitution? Reason and argument? You might as well reason and argue with the marble columns encircling them. The representatives chosen by ourselves? They are joined in the combination, some from incorrect views of government, some from corrupt ones, sufficient voting together to outnumber the sound parts; and with majorities only of one, two, or three, bold enough to go forward in defiance.

That is why we are having the Revolution of 2016, as you did in the second revolution of 1800. Representatives and elected officials are not representing the citizens, but each other, themselves, and their special interests.

Are we then to stand to our arms, with the hot-headed * * * ? No. That must be the last resource, not to be thought of until much longer and greater sufferings. If every infraction of a compact of so many parties is to be resisted at once, as a dissolution of it, none can ever be formed which would last one year.

We must have patience and longer endurance then with our brethren while under delusion; give them time for reflection and experience of consequences; keep ourselves in a situation to profit by the chapter of accidents; and separate from our companions only when the sole alternatives left, are the dissolution of our Union with them, or submission to a government without limitation of powers. Between these two evils, when we must make a choice, there can be no hesitation.

But, in the meanwhile, the States should be watchful to note every material usurpation on their rights; denounce them as they occur in the most peremptory terms; to protest against them as wrongs to which our present submission shall be considered, not as acknowledgments or precedents of right, but as a temporary yielding to the lesser evil, until their accumulation shall overweigh that of separation. I would go still further, and give to the Federal member, by a regular amendment of the Constitution, a right to make roads and canals of intercommunication between the States, providing sufficiently against corrupt practices in Congress by declaring that the Federal proportion of each State of the moneys so employed, shall be in works within the State, or elsewhere with its consent, and with a due salvo of jurisdiction. This is the course which I think safest and best as yet.[116]

Unfortunately, most of the States do not take on the Federal Government to protect their rights, or our rights. Perhaps one day it will be bad enough to have an Article Five Convention of States to hopefully correct the ills of our nation.

The example of changing a constitution by assembling the wise men of the State, instead of assembling armies, will be worth as much to the world as the former examples we had given them.[117]

Some men look at constitutions with sanctimonious

---

[116] To William B. Giles #1183 (M., Dec. 1825.)
[117] To David Humphreys #1795 (P., 1789.)

reverence, and deem them like the ark of the covenant, too sacred to be touched. They ascribe to the men of the preceding age a wisdom more than human, and suppose what they did to be beyond amendment. I knew that age well: I belonged to it, and labored with it. It deserved well of its country. It was very like the present, but without the experience of the present; and forty years of experience in government is worth a century of book reading; and this they would say themselves, were they to rise from the dead.

So you agree with me that if the Constitution needs fixing, it may be through amendments in an orderly fashion.

I am certainly not an advocate for frequent and untried changes in laws and constitutions. I think moderate imperfections had better be borne with; because, when once known, we accommodate ourselves to them and find practical means of correcting their ill effects.

But I know, also, that laws and institutions must go hand in hand with the progress of the human mind. As that becomes more developed, more enlightened, as new discoveries are made, new truths disclosed, and manners and opinions change with the change of circumstances, institutions must advance also, and keep pace with the times. We might as well require a man to wear still the coat which fitted him when a boy, as civilized society to remain ever under the regimen of their barbarous ancestors.

It is this preposterous idea which has lately deluged Europe in blood. Their monarchs, instead of wisely yielding to the gradual change of circumstances, of favoring progressive accommodation to progressive improvement, have clung to old abuses, entrenched themselves behind steady habits, and obliged their subjects to seek through blood and violence rash and ruinous innovations, which, had they been referred to the peaceful deliberations and collected wisdom of the nation, would have been put into acceptable and salutary forms.

Let us follow no such examples, nor weakly believe that one generation is not as capable as another of taking care of itself, and of ordering its own affairs.

* * * That majority, then, has a right to depute representatives to a convention, and to make the constitution what they think will be the best for themselves. * * * If this avenue be shut to the call of sufferance, it will make itself heard through that of force, and we shall go on, as other nations are doing, in the endless circle of oppression, rebellion, reformation; and oppression, rebellion, reformation, again; and so on forever.[118]

Education is the true corrective of abuses of constitutional power.[119]

---

[118] To Samuel Kerchival #1733 (M., 1816.)
[119] To William C. Jarvis #6816 (M., 1820.)

That is true, but it depends on who provides the education. It would be on the opposite ends of the spectrum should we learn from President Obama, or if we learn from former Speaker, Newt Gingrich. In Colorado, some of their advanced placement texts do not even mention the founders.

Hitherto I have been under the guidance of that portion of reason which God has thought proper to deal out to me. I have followed it faithfully in all important cases, to such a degree at least as leaves me without uneasiness; and if on minor occasions I have erred from its dictates, I have trust in Him who made us what we are, and I know it was not His plan to make us always unerring.[120]

Mr. Jefferson over the last years, Congress, the President and the Supreme Court have not questioned the authority of what the other is doing. We are ending up with Executive Orders of the President, the nationalization of the health care, the overstepping of bounds. I believe it is not the way the Founders had planned for our government to be.

When all government, domestic and foreign, in little as in great things, shall be drawn to Washington as the centre of all power, it will render powerless the checks provided of one government on another, and will become as venal and oppressive as the government from which we separated.[121] *I wish to see maintained that wholesome distribution of powers established by the Constitution for the limitation of both;*

[120] To Miles King #7258 (M., 1814.)
[121] To C. Hammond #1184 (M., 1821.)

and never to see all offices transferred to Washington, where, further with drawn from the eyes of the people, they may more secretly be bought and sold as at market.[122]

I said to [President Washington] that if the equilibrium of the three great bodies, Legislative, Executive, and Judiciary, could be preserved, if the Legislature could be kept independent, I should never fear the result of such a government; but that I could not but be uneasy when I saw that the Executive had swallowed up the Legislative branch.[123] I look for our safety to the broad representation of the people [in Congress]. It will be more difficult for corrupt views to lay hold of so large a mass.[124]

What did you do when a branch of the government overstepped their authority?

Where powers are assumed which have not been delegated, a nullification of the act is the rightful remedy.[125] If the three powers [of our government] maintain their mutual independence on each other it may last long, but not so if either can assume the authorities of the other.[126]

Then what are we to do?

---

[122] To William Johnson #1160 (M., 1823.)
[123] The Anas #1161   (1792.)
[124] To T. M. Randolph #1565 (Pa., 1792.)
[125] Kentucky Resolutions #6847 (1798.)
[126] To William C. Jarvis #2924 (M., 1820.)

The only hope of safety hangs now on the numerous representation which is to come forward the ensuing year. Some of the new members will be, probably, either in principle or interest, with the present majority, but it is expected that the great mass will form an accession to the republican party. They will not be able to undo all which the two preceding Legislatures, and especially the first, have done. Public faith and right will oppose this. But some parts of the system may be rightfully reformed, a liberation from the rest unremittingly pursued as fast as right will permit, and the door shut in future against similar commitments of the nation.[127] *Let us then go on perfecting it, by adding, by way of amendment to the Constitution those powers which time and trial show are still wanting.*[128]

Where can we learn more about how the Constitution should be viewed?

*Colonel Taylor's book of "Constructions Construed" * * * is the most logical retraction of our governments to the original and true principles of the Constitution creating them, which has appeared since the adoption of that instrument. I may not perhaps concur in all its opinions, great and small, for no two men ever thought alike on so many points. But on all important questions, it contains the true political faith, to which every catholic republican should steadfastly hold. It should be put into the hands of all our functionaries,*

---

[127] To President Washington #1566 (Pa., May 1792.)
[128] To Wilson C. Nicholas #1667 (M., Sep. 1803.)

authoritatively, as a standing instruction and true exposition of our Constitution, as understood at the time we agreed to it.[129]

Let us look on to Congress.

---

[129] To Spencer Roane #8362 (M., 1821.)

On The Congress

Action by the citizens in person, in affairs within their reach and competence, and in all others by representatives, chosen immediately, and removable by themselves, constitutes the essence of a republic.[130]

To expend the public money with the same care and economy [that] we would practice with our own [is one of] the land marks by which we are to guide ourselves in all our proceedings.[131]

It seems to us common citizens, that the United States may still be the best place to live, but we are in a serious mess. Looking at the three branches of government, let us visit about Congress first. I would say we are closest to the Senators and Representatives as they are from our districts and state.

---

[130] To Dupont de Nemours #7300 (P.F., 1816.)
[131] Second Annual Message #2355 (Dec. 1802.)

I think it a duty in those entrusted with the administration of their affairs to conform themselves to the decided choice of their constituents.[132]

You mean it is not the Congressman knows best, that they should represent the people from their district or state that voted them in? Congress has had the Contract with America. Maybe Congressmen and Senators should have a contract with their voters. One thing that I believe should be done, is that if the Federal Government is going to continue to heap rules, regulations and programs on the states, then the United State Senators should be selected by the state legislatures, as the Constitution was originally established, so they can protect the states from federal abuse.

*The Constitution of the United States * * * [has] delegated to Congress a power to punish treason, counterfeiting the securities and current coin of the United States, piracies, and felonies committed on the high seas, and offences against the law of nations, and no other crimes whatsoever; and it being true as a general principle, and one of the amendments to the Constitution having also declared, that "the powers not delegated to the United States by the Constitution, nor prohibited by it to the States, are reserved to the States respectively, or to the people" * * * the power to create, define, and punish * * * other crimes is reserved, and of right, appertains solely and exclusively to the respective States, each within its own territory.*[133]

---

[132] To John Jay #1576 (P., 1785.)
[133] Kentucky Resolutions #6838 (1798.)

There are 194,000 federal inmates. It seems that the states must have turned over a lot of authority to Congress. Over the last years Congress has been weak, allowing the President to do as he pleases, allowing the Courts to legislate, and spending like there is no tomorrow. We need leadership and planning. They have long overstepped their authority.

In the early 1990's, the Contract with America was a great example of planning, developed by Newt Gingrich, who became Speaker of the House and Dick Armey, who became House Majority Leader. As an agreement with the citizens, the Republicans would do specific things if they were elected and reelected. Because of the trust the voters had with the Contract with America, they elected a Republican Congress. It gave the citizens some idea for a plan of the United States. The republicans won control of the legislature. It was successful, even though President Clinton vetoed some of the proposals as well as the House and Senate not supporting some of it.

You now see the composition of our public bodies, and how essential system and plan are for conducting our affairs wisely with so bitter a party in opposition to us, who look not at all to what is best for the public, but how they may thwart whatever we may propose, though they should thereby sink their country.[134]

As time went on, Congress again lost its power, or should I say, they did not lose their power, but chose not to enforce their power.

---

[134] To Caeser A. Rodney #1561 (W., 1804.)

*The authority of Congress can never be wounded without injury to the present Union.[135] Congress * * * [is] not a party but merely the creature of the [Federal] compact, and [is] subject, as to its assumptions of power, to the final judgment of those by whom, and for whose use, itself and its powers were all created and modified.[136]*

We have so many politicians in Congress, with their elections costing so much to run for office, they learned that they could retain office for a long time by concentrating on raising campaign funds rather than concentrating on good government policy. Former Georgia Senator Zell Miller, a Democrat, complained of this. He supported Republican George W. Bush for President and left the Senate, not seeking re-election

We want men of business [in Congress]. * * I am convinced it is in the power of any man who understands business, and who will undertake to keep a file of the business before Congress and press it, as he would his own docket in a court, to shorten the sessions a month one year with another, and to save in that way * * * An ill-judged modesty prevents those from undertaking it who are equal to it.[137] Enough wealthy men will find their way into every branch of the legislature to protect themselves.[138]*

---

[135] To the President of Congress #1505 (Wg., 1779.)
[136] Kentucky Resolutions #1513 (1798.)
[137] To Caeser A. Rodney #1508 (W., Dec. 1802.)
[138] To John Adams #9054 (M., 1813.)

Congress, rather than pass a timely budget, passes continuing resolutions to temporarily fund government operations, instead of shutting down the government. The government is in so many parts of American lives, Congress cannot keep up on all the programs and budgets. Authorizations for programs may have lapsed, but still get funded. Congress is afraid of a showdown and a shutdown, with the presidential veto.

It will be forever seen that of bodies of men even elected by the people, there will always be a greater proportion aristocratic than among their constituents.[139]

As Americans are looking at the fundamental change in the Executive office in the upcoming election, what about Congress? We had a strong conservative movement in Congress in the 1990's, after President Reagan started it in the 1980's. Is there a chance of us getting it again with this election?

There is a snail-paced gait for the advance of new ideas on the general mind, under which we must acquiesce. A forty years experience of popular assemblies has taught me, that you must give them time for every step you take. If too hard pushed, they balk, and the machine retrogrades.[140]

*We shall push Congress to the uttermost in economizing.[141] I think it an object of great importance. * * * to simplify our system of finance, and bring it within*

---

[139] To Benjamin Hawkins #7268 (W., 1803.)
[140] To Joel Barlow #7018 (W., Dec. 1807.)
[141] To Nathaniel Macon #2361 (W., May 1801.)

the comprehension of every member of Congress.[142]
*There never was a time when the services of those
who possess talents, integrity, firmness, and sound
judgment, were more wanted in Congress. Some one of
that description is particularly wanted to take the
lead in the House of Representatives, to consider the
business of the nation as his own business, to take it
up as if he were singly charged with it, and carry it
through.*

*I do not mean that any gentleman, relinquishing his
own judgment, should implicitly support all the
measures of the administration; but that, where he
does not disapprove of them, he should not suffer
them to go off in sleep, but bring them to the attention of the House, and give them a fair chance. Where
he disapproves, he will of course leave them to be
brought forward by those who concur in the sentiment.*[143]

*It [is] a cause of just uneasiness, when we [see] a legis-
lature legislating for their own interests, in opposition to those of the people.*[144] *Political interest can
never be separated in the long run from moral
right.*[145]

It seems to us novices, that Congress makes the law, but in
fact, at least in the present era, that the Executive Branch,
makes the actual rules and whether the rules and laws are

---

[142] To Albert Gallatin #3005 (W., April 1802.)
[143] To Mr. Bidwell #1545 (W., 1806.)
[144] The Anas #1519 (1792.)
[145] To James Monroe #6740 (W., 1806.)

enforced. A couple of good examples are the Administration's rules on immigration and the rules putting the coal industry out of business.

Laws are made for men of ordinary understanding, and should therefore, be construed by the ordinary rules of common sense. Their meaning is not to be sought for in metaphysical subtleties, which may make anything mean everything or nothing, at pleasure.[146] The execution of the laws is more important than the making them.[147]

The republicans complain that the influence and patronage of the Executive are to become so great as to govern the Legislature.[148] Whatever of the enumerated objects [in the Constitution] is proper for a law, Congress may make the law.[149]

The President did just get hammered by the Supreme Court on not enforcing the immigration laws, but there is so much more.

The patronage of public office should no longer be confided to one who uses it for active opposition to the national will.[150]

Oh my, President Obama is constantly in opposition to the national will.

---

146 To William Johnson #4524 (M., 1823.)
147 To M. L'Abbé Arnold #4494 (P., 1789.)
148 To Thomas Pickney #1530 (Pa., 1792.)
149 To Wilson C. Nicholas #1547 (M., 1803.)
150 To Albert Gallatin #6474 (1804.)

In the construction of a law, even in judiciary cases of meum et tuum [mine and thine] where the opposite parties have a right and counter-right in the very words of the law, the judge considers the intention of the law giver as his true guide, and gives to all the parts and expressions of the law, that meaning which will effect, instead of defeating, its intention. But in laws merely executive, where no private right stands in the way, and the public object is the interest of all, a much freer scope of construction, in favor of the intention of the law, ought to be taken, and ingenuity ever should be exercised in devising constructions, which may save to the public the benefit of the law. Its intention is the important thing: the means of attaining it quite subordinate.

It often happens that, the Legislature prescribing the details of execution, some circumstance arises unforeseen or unattended to by them, which would totally frustrate their intention, were their details scrupulously adhered to, and deemed exclusive of all others.

But constructions must not be favored which go to defeat instead of furthering the principal object of the law, and to sacrifice the end to the means. It being as evidently their intention that the end shall be attained as that it should be effected by any given means, if both cannot be observed, we are equally free to deviate from the one as the other, and more rational in postponing the means to the end.

* * * It is further to be considered that the Constitution gives the Executive a general power to carry the laws into execution. If the present law had enacted that the service of 30,000 volunteers should be accepted, without saying anything of the means, those means would, by the Constitution, have resulted to the discretion of the Executive.

So if means specified by an act are impracticable, the constitutional power remains and supplies them. Often the means provided specially are affirmative merely, and, with the constitutional powers, stand well together; so that either may be used, or the one supplementary to the other. This aptitude of means to the end of a law is essentially necessary for those which are executive; otherwise the objection that our government is an impracticable one, would really be verified.[151]

It seems you are saying that Congress needs to define the laws more if they do not want the Administration to make up the rules. They do not need to make more laws, such as on guns, when the current laws are not enforced.

A full representation at the ensuing session [of Congress] will doubtless * * * take measures for ensuring the authority of the laws over the corrupt maneuvers of the heads of departments under the pretext of exercising discretion in opposition to law.[152]

---

[151] To W. H. Cabell #4483 (M., Aug. 1807.)
[152] To T. M. Randolph #2235 (Pa., 1793.)

*The Executive * * * has the power, though not the right, to apply money contrary to its legal appropriations. Cases may be imagined, however, where it would be their duty to do this. But they must be cases of extreme necessity. The payment of interest the domestic creditors has been mentioned as one of the causes of diverting the foreign fund. But this is not an object of greater necessity than that to which it was legally appropriated. It is taking the money from our foreign creditors to pay it to the domestic ones; a preference which neither justice, gratitude, nor the estimation in which these two descriptions of creditors are held in this country will justify. The payment of the Army and the daily expenses of the government have been also mentioned as objects of withdrawing this money. These indeed are pressing objects, and might produce that degree of distressing necessity which would be a justification.[153]*

The trouble now a days, the legislative bills are large and are not read by the legislators. Obamacare legislation is a great example. It was thousands of pages and Congress was forced to vote on it by the House and Senate leadership without the time to read and study it. The Speaker of the House at the time, Nancy Pelosi said there would be plenty of time to read it after it was passed. Billions of dollars in expenses.

Delay is preferable to error.[154] [Reformation] must be brought about by the people, using their elective

---

[153] To President Washington #419 (Pa., 1793.)
[154] To George Washington, LOC May 16, 1792
http://hdl.loc.gov/loc.mss/mtj.mtjbib006165

rights with prudence and self-possession, and not suffering themselves to be duped by treacherous emissaries.[155] Things even salutary should not be crammed down the throats of dissenting brethren, especially when they may be put into a form to be willingly swallowed.[156]

The instability of our laws is really an immense evil. I think it would be well to provide in our constitutions that there shall always be a twelve month between the engrossing a bill and passing it; that it should then be offered to its passage without changing a word; and that if circumstances should be thought to require a speedier passage, it should take two-thirds of both Houses, instead of a bare majority.[157]

When the Obamacare issue went before the Supreme Court, the court upheld both Obamacare and the Tax Credits the law provided. Judge Roberts was assailed in his decision, but I believe, based on what you are saying, the court should expand instead of defeating the law. Roberts was correct in his decision. Congress should not have passed it.

Constructions which do not result from the words of the Legislator, but lie hidden in his breast, till called forth, ex post facto, by subsequent occasions, are dangerous and not to be justified by ordinary emergencies.[158] The Legislative and executive branches may

---

155 To Arthur Campbell #7198 (M., 1797.)
156 To Edward Livingston #7193 (M., 1824.)
157 To James Madison #4506 (P., 1787.)
158 Report to Congress #4480 (1778.)

sometimes err, but elections and dependence will bring them to rights.[159]

Our current Speaker of the House, Paul Ryan, wanted a repeal of one of your Rules before he would run for Speaker of the House, it was the provision giving members of the House the power to replace the sitting Speaker. He ended up dropping that demand before running for the position. The demand was due to the House voting out the previous Speaker.

Men of energy of character must have enemies; because there are two sides to every question, and taking one with decision, and acting on it with effect, those who take the other will of course be hostile in proportion as they feel that effect.[160] *Should things go wrong at any time, the people will set them to rights by the peaceable exercise of their elective rights.*[161]

I had hoped that the proceedings of this session of Congress would have rallied the great body of our citizens at once to one opinion. But the inveteracy of their quondam leaders has been able by intermingling the grossest lies and misrepresentations to check the effect in some small degree until they shall be exposed. The great sources and authors of these are in Congress.[162]

Regrettably, when the Republican Party had an agreement with the presidential candidates, that the winner of the primaries

---

[159] To Archibald Thweat #2439 (M., 1821.)
[160] To John Adams #2606 (M., 1817.)
[161] To Wilson C. Nicholas #2427 (W., 1806.)
[162] To Caeser A. Rodney #1563 (W., April 1802.)

would be supported by the other candidates, the powers to be did not expect Donald Trump, a businessman instead of a politician, to be selected in the primaries. The agreement was dissolved months before the convention so no one had an agreement to support the winner. Even so, Ted Cruz was invited to the Republican Convention, but did not endorse Trump. It appears he would rather have Hillary Clinton win so he has a chance to run in four years.

*Some [members of Congress] think that independence requires them to follow always their own opinion, without respect for that of others. This has never been my opinion, nor my practice, when I have been of that or any other body. Differing, on a particular question, from those whom I knew to be of the same political principles with myself, and with whom I generally thought and acted, a consciousness of the fallibility of the human mind, and of my own in particular, with a respect for the accumulated judgment of my friends, has induced me to suspect erroneous impressions in myself, to suppose my own opinion wrong, and to act with them on theirs. The want of this spirit of compromise, or of self-distrust, proudly, but falsely called independence, is what gives the federalists victories which they could never obtain, if these brethren could learn to respect the opinions of their friends more than of their enemies, and prevents many able and honest men from doing all the good they otherwise might do. These considerations * * * have often quieted my own conscience in voting* *and acting on the judgment of others against my own.*[163]

Jeb Bush is another candidate not endorsing Trump. John Kasick was the third major candidate, hiding out, not supporting the party, and how embarrassing for Kasick not to go to the Republican Convention in his home state. To not support the Republican nominee gives the citizens the appearance that he supports the Democrat. That means something in the Republican Party and it will negatively affect the former presidential candidates in any future national race.

Good faith ought ever to be the rule of action in public as well as in private transactions.[164] *Good faith is every man's surest guide.*[165] *If we do not learn to sacrifice small differences of opinion, we can never act together. Every man cannot have his way in all things. If his own opinion prevails at some times, he should acquiesce on seeing that of others preponderate at other times. Without this mutual disposition we are disjointed individuals, but not a society.*[166]

The times do certainly render it incumbent on all good citizens, attached to the rights and honor of their country, to bury in oblivion all internal differences, and rally around the standard of their country in opposition to the outrages of foreign nations. All attempts to enfeeble and destroy the exertions of the General Government, in vindication of our national

[163] To William Duane #6209 (M., 1811.)
[164] Sixth Annual Message #2855 (1806.)
[165] Peace Proclamation #2856 (1784.)
[166] To John Dickinson #6237 (W., July 1801.)

rights, or to loosen the bands of Union by alienating the affections of the people, or opposing the authority of the laws at so eventful a period, merit the discountenance of all.[167]

In some of the past presidencies, we have had the Presidents enriching themselves after leaving office. The Clinton's said they were broke when leaving the White House, and in 2015, lists their wealth as $111 million dollars. Donald Trump, a successful businessman, shows his wealth in the billions, before seeking office, and is not looking for personal gain.

Bringing into office no desires of making it subservient to the advancement of my own private interests, it has been no sacrifice, by postponing them, to strengthen the confidence of my fellow citizens.[168]

In a government like ours, it is the duty of the Chief Magistrate, in order to enable himself to do all the good which his station requires, to endeavor, by all honorable means, to unite in himself the confidence of the whole people. This alone, in any case where the energy of the nation is required, can produce a union of the powers of the whole, and point them in a single direction, as if all constituted but one body and one mind; and this alone can render a weaker nation unconquerable by a stronger one. Towards acquiring the confidence of the people, the very first measure is to satisfy them of his disinterestedness, and that he is

---

[167] To Governor Tompkins #8726 (Feb. 1809.)
[168] To Horation Turpin #7105 (W., 1807.)

directing their affairs with a single eye to their good, and not to build up fortunes for himself and family.[169]

We have seen leaders of foreign nations address Congress, including, most recently Israeli Prime Minister Benjamin Netanyahu, Japanese Prime Minister Shinzo Abe, Vatican City Sovereign Pope Francis and India Prime Minister Narendra Modi.

The Legislature should never show itself in a matter with a foreign nation, but where the case is very serious, and they mean to commit the nation on its issue.[170] The Executive of the Union is, by the Constitution, made the channel of communication between foreign powers and the United States. But citizens, whether individually, or in bodies corporate, or associated, have a right to apply directly to any department of their government, whether Legislative, Executive, or Judiciary, the exercise of whose powers they have a right to claim; and neither of these can regularly offer its intervention in a case belonging to the other. [171]

In the current presidential election, the Republican nominee, Donald Trump, wants to, if elected, to keep Muslims from coming to the United States until a good screening process for terrorists is developed. Trump wants them thoroughly vetted and they should not be placed in front of those in line for citizenship. He also wants to exclude illegal immigrants, the movement to the United States. According to the Constitution, naturalization is a power of Congress on how a person

---

[169] To J. Garland Jefferson #7096 (M., 1810.)
[170] To James Madison #1534 (1791.)
[171] To James Sullivan #6648 (W., 1807.)

may become a citizen.

Congress may, by the Constitution, "establish an uniform rule of naturalization," that is, by what rule an alien may become a citizen.[172]

* * * to produce rapid population by as great importations of foreigners as possible. But is this founded in good policy? * * * It is for the happiness of those united in society to harmonize as much as possible in matters which they must of necessity transact together. Civil government being the sole object of forming societies, its administration must be conducted by common consent.

We should be wary of those coming into our country. When they come in mass, as has been happening with refugees, the problem of them following our laws rather than their former countries laws has become an issue.

Every species of government has its specific principles. Ours perhaps are more peculiar than those of any other in the universe. It is a composition of the freest principles of the English constitution, with others derived from natural right and natural reason. To these nothing can be more opposed than the maxims of absolute monarchies. Yet from such we are to expect the greatest number of emigrants. They will bring with them the principles of the governments they leave, imbibed in their early youth; or, if able to throw them off, it will be in exchange for an

---

[172] To Albert Gallatin #2837 (W., June 1806.)

unbounded licentiousness, passing, as is usual, from one extreme to another. It would be a miracle were they to stop precisely at the point of temperate liberty.

These principles, with their language, they will transmit to their children. In proportion to their numbers, they will share with us the legislation. They will infuse into it their spirit, warp and bias its directions, and render it a heterogeneous, incoherent, distracted mass. I may appeal to experience, during the present contest, for a verification of these conjectures. But, if they be not certain in event, are they not possible, are they not probable?

So you believe we should follow our laws on immigration?

* * * May not our government be more homogeneous, more peaceable, more durable? Suppose twenty millions of republican Americans thrown all of a sudden into France, what would be the condition of that kingdom? If it would be more turbulent, less happy, less strong, we may believe that the addition of half a million of foreigners to our present numbers would produce a similar effect here. If they come of themselves they are entitled to all the rights of citizenship; but I doubt the expediency of inviting them by extraordinary encouragements.[173]

Those coming legally, to the United States, follow our laws, and may be able to become a citizen. We also have a large number of illegal immigrants, those who do not follow our

---

[173] Notes on Virginia #3845 (1782.)

laws of entry. The government is not following the laws in expelling the illegal ones.

No government [can] discharge its duties to the best advantage of its citizens, if its agents [are] in a regular course of thwarting instead of executing all its measures, and [are] employing the patronage and influence of their offices against the government and its measures.[174]

As to other [than English] foreigners, it is thought better to discourage their settling together in large masses, wherein, as in our German settlements, they preserve for a long time their own languages, habits and principles of government, and that they should distribute themselves sparsely among the natives for quicker amalgamation. English emigrants are without this inconvenience. They differ from us little but in their principles of government, and most of those (merchants excepted) who come here, are sufficiently disposed to adopt ours.[175]

*The papers from the free people * * * I apprehend it will be best to take no notice of. They are parties in a domestic quarrel, which, I think, we should leave to be settled among themselves.*[176]

What about the Muslims? In the early years you pushed for a freedom for all religions.

---

174 To John Page #6475 (W., July 1807.)
175 To George Fowler #3833 (P.F., 1817)
176 To President Washington #3840 (Pa., 1791.)

With the religion of other countries my own forbids intermeddling.[177]

Did your views change on Islam later on, after the establishment of our nation? You had considerable trouble with Islamic countries before and during your presidency.

An enemy generally says and believes what he wishes.[178] *We took the liberty to make some inquiries concerning the Grounds of their pretentions to make war upon Nations who had done them no Injury, and observed that we considered all mankind as our friends who had done us no wrong, nor had given us any provocation.*

The Ambassador answered us that it was founded on the Laws of their Prophet, that it was written in their Koran, that all nations who should not have acknowledged their authority were sinners, that it was their right and duty to make war upon them wherever they could be found, and to make slaves of all they could take as Prisoners, and that every Musselman [Muslim] who should be slain in battle was sure to go to Paradise.[179]

That was ten years after the Declaration of Independence. You also had comments about Islamic Turkey.

---

[177] To Samuel Greenhow #7241 (M., 1814.)
[178] To C. W. F. Dumas #2600 (A., 1788.)
[179] T. Jefferson & J. Adams to John Jay, LOC, March 28, 1786
http://hdl.loc.gov/loc.mss/mtj.mtjbib001849

It has been thought that the two imperial courts [Austria and Russia] have a plan of expelling the Turks from Europe. It is really a pity so charming a country should remain in the hands of a people, whose religion forbids the admission of science and the arts among them. We should wish success to the object of the two empires, if they meant to leave the country in possession of the Greek inhabitants. We might then expect, once more, to see the language of Homer and Demosthenes a living language. For I am persuaded the modern Greek would easily get back to its classical models. But this is not intended. They only propose to put the Greeks under other masters; to substitute one set of barbarians for another.[180]

I cannot think but that it would be desirable to all commercial nations to have Turkey and all its dependencies driven from the seacoast into the interior parts of Asia and Africa. What a field would thus be restored to commerce! The finest parts of the old world are now dead in a great degree to commerce, to arts, to sciences, and to society. Greece, Syria, Egypt, and the northern coast of Africa, constituted the whole world almost for the Romans, and to us they are scarcely known, scarcely accessible at all.[181]

I have long lamented the depreciation of law science. The opinion seems to be that Blackstone is to us what the Alkoran is to the Mahometans, that everything

---

[180] To Dr. Stiles #8623 (P., 1785.)
[181] To John Brown #8626 (P., 1788.)

which is necessary is in him; and what is not in him is not necessary.[182]

You desire the Muslims to be run off by Russia and Austria, and would like them moved from the Mediterranean shores. It appears you would not want them here. As we looked to Blackstone for our laws, the Muslims look to the Koran for theirs, so it seems you may have a problem with the losing of science and the arts, as well as their right to make war on us. We have the war on terror now, and they are Muslims. Did your views of religion change from the Founding era of our country?

One of our fan-coloring biographers, who paints small men as very great, enquired of me lately, with real affection, too, whether he might consider as authentic, the change in my religion much spoken of in some circles. Now this supposed that they knew what had been my religion before, taking for it the word of their priests, whom I certainly never made the confidants of my creed. My answer was, "say nothing of my religion. It is known to my God and myself alone. Its evidence before the world is to be sought in my life; if that has been honest and dutiful to society, the religion which has regulated it cannot be a bad one".[183]

I believe your views of the Muslim religion did change. How we wander. We may come back to religion later on, but let us

---

[182] To John Tyler #4544 (M., 1810.)
[183] To John Adams #7252 (M., 1817.)

get back to the government issues. It seems that Congress is in session all year, your comments?

Each house of Congress possesses the natural right of governing itself, and, consequently, of fixing its own times and places of meeting, so far as it has not been abridged by the law of those who employ them, that is to say, by the Constitution.[184]

I was in hopes that all efforts to render the sessions of Congress permanent were abandoned. But a clear profit of * * * a day is sufficient to reconcile some to their absence from home.[185] *To shorten the sessions, is to lessen the evils and burthens of the government on our country.*[186]

Most of the American citizenry, it seems, pays little attention to what Congress does unless it is an issue of their personal concern. Congress has many votes on an issue, so when the representative runs for reelection, the representative can say, and quote a vote that they made, either for or against some part of the legislation. Many of them are blowing in the wind.

I observe that the House of Representatives are sensible of the ill effects of the long speeches in their house on their proceedings. But they have a worse effect in the disgust they excite among the people, and the disposition they are producing to transfer their confidence from the Legislature to the Executive branch, which would soon sap our Constitution. These speeches,

---

[184] Official Opinion #1586 (1790.)
[185] To James Madison #1588 (1798.)
[186] To James Monroe #1587 (Pa., 1798.)

therefore, are less and less read, and if continued will soon cease to be read at all.[187] *I served with General Washington in the Legislature of Virginia before the Revolution and, during it, with Dr. Franklin in Congress. I never heard either of them speak ten minutes at a time, nor to any but the main point which was to decide the question. They laid their shoulders to the great points, knowing that the little ones would follow of themselves.*[188]

The Founding Fathers must have had great command of the language, to get to the point. Mr. Jefferson, I know Congress has the responsibility of taxation, but I would ask that we defer that subject until later. What do you thing about the "sit in protest" in the House of Representatives? Minority Leader Pelosi and Democrat Congressmen having a hissy fit over gun control.

I may err in my measures, but never shall deflect from the Intention to fortify the public liberty by every possible means, and to put it out of the power of the few to riot on the labors of the many.[189] * * * *it is their [the citizens] right and duty to be at all times armed; that they are entitled to freedom of person, freedom of religion, freedom of property, and freedom of the press.*[190]

Mr. Jefferson, what do you think about the Senate's rule requiring 60 votes to pass an issue?

---

[187] John Wayles Eppes #1598 (M., 1810.)
[188] Autobiography #1993 (1821.)
[189] To Judge Tyler #4316 (W., 1804.)
[190] To John Cartwright #1728 (M., 1824.)

*A nation ceases to be republican * * * when the will of the majority ceases to be the law.[191] Truth advances, and error recedes step by step only; and to do our fellow-men the most good in our power, we must lead where we can, follow where we cannot, and still go with them, watching always the favorable moment for helping them to another step.[192]*

Any other words of wisdom for Congress before we move on to the President's position?

Economy in the public expense, that labor may be lightly burdened, I deem [one of the] essential principles of our government and, consequently [one] which ought to shape its administration.[193]

The power to regulate commerce does not give a power to build piers, wharves, open ports, clear the beds of rivers, dig canals, build warehouses, build manufacturing machines, set up manufactories, cultivate the earth, to all of which the power would go if it went to the first.[194]

In stating prudential rules for our government in society, I must not omit the important one of never entering into dispute or argument with another. I never saw an instance of one of two disputants convincing the other by argument. I have seen many, on their getting warm, becoming rude, and shooting one

191 Reply to Address #7330 (W., 1808.)
192 To Thomas Cooper #7192 (M., 1814.)
193 First Inaugural Address #4305 (1801.)
194 To Albert Gallatin #6854 (1802.)

another. Conviction is the effect of our own dispassionate reasoning, either in solitude, or weighing within ourselves, dispassionately, what we hear from others, standing uncommitted in argument ourselves. It was one of the rules which, above all others, made Dr. Franklin the most amiable of men in society, "never to contradict anybody." If he was urged to announce an opinion, he did it rather by asking questions, as if for information, or by suggesting doubts.

When I hear another express an opinion which is not mine, I say to myself, he has a right to his opinion, as I to mine; why should I question it? His error does me no injury, and shall I become a Don Quixote, to bring all men by force of argument to one opinion? If a fact be misstated, it is probable he is gratified by a belief of it, and I have no right to deprive him of the gratification. If he wants information, he will ask it, and then I will give it in measured terms; but if he still believes his own story, and shows a desire to dispute the fact with me, I hear him and say nothing. It is his affair, not mine, if he prefers error.[195]

I have but one system of ethics for men and for nations to be grateful, to be faithful to all engagements, under all circumstances, to be open and generous, promoting in the long run the interests of both, and I am sure it promotes their happiness.[196]

---

[195] To Thomas Jefferson Randolph #2242 (W., 1808.)
[196] To La Duchesse D'Auville #3598 (N.Y. 1790.)

On The Presidency

As to the portions of power within each State assigned to the General Government, the President is as much the Executive of the State, as their particular governor is in relation to State powers.[197]

A concern, in this election as in many past, is the idea of electors and the electoral college.

The President is chosen by ourselves, directly in practice, for we vote for A as elector only on the condition he will vote for B.[198]

In a hotly contested election, in an evenly divided country as we have today, even though the elector pledges to vote as the citizens did, it is not required by law.

---

[197] To Mr. Goodenow #6892 (M., 1822.)
[198] To Dupont de Nemours #6874 (P.F., 1816.)

The contrivance in the Constitution for marking the votes works badly, because it does not enounce precisely the true expression of the public will.[199]

You served eight years as President after four years as Vice President, so please discuss the issues of the Executive Branch of government.

The second office of the government is honorable and easy; the first is but a splendid misery.[200]

Mr. Jefferson, what a difference in the attitude between the Vice President, who is the President of the Senate, and the President positions. As Vice President, you...

As to duty, the Constitution will know me only as the member of the Legislative body; and its principle is, that of a separation of Legislative, Executive and Judiciary functions, except in cases specified. If this principle be not expressed in direct terms, it is clearly the spirit of the Constitution and it ought to be so commented and acted on by every friend of free government.[201] *The Senate is not supposed by the Constitution to be acquainted with the concerns of the Executive department. It was not intended that these should be communicated to them.*[202]

The job of the President?

---

[199] To Tench Coxe #6899 (W., Dec. 1800.)
[200] To Elbridge Gerry. #8811 (Pa., 1797.)
[201] To James Madison #8810 (M., Jan. 1797.)
[202] Opinion on the Powers of the Senate #6890 (1790.)

To cultivate peace and maintain commerce and navigation in all their lawful enterprises; to foster our fisheries and nurseries of navigation and for the nurture of man, and protect the manufactures adapted to our circumstances; to preserve the faith of the nation by an exact discharge of its debts and contracts, expending the public money with the same care and economy we would practice with our own, and impose on our citizens no unnecessary burden; to keep in all things within the pale of our constitutional powers, and cherish the Federal Union as the only rock of our safety these are the land marks by which we are to guide ourselves in all our proceedings. By continuing to make these our rule of action, we shall endear to our countrymen the true principles of their Constitution, and promote a union of sentiment and of action equally auspicious to their happiness and safety.[203]

If the Presidents would only do that, they might have even more time to play golf. Who would take care of our healthcare, our transportation, our environment?

There was but a single act of my whole administration of which the federal party approved. That was the proclamation on the attack of the Chesapeake. And when I found they approved of it, I confess I began strongly to apprehend I had done wrong, and to exclaim with the Psalmist, "Lord, what have I done that the wicked should praise me."[204]

---

[203] Second Annual Message #123 (1802.)
[204] To Elbridge Gerry #117 (M., 1812.)

That's pretty funny, for such a great man to be despised so. The United States would definitely be different had you been the second President. The Federalist ways would not have been entrenched into the government fabric. You did end up supporting Adams to be the second President.

It seems possible, that the Representatives may be divided. This is a difficulty from which the Constitution has provided no issue. It is both my duty and inclination, therefore, to relieve the embarrassment, should it happen: and in that case, I pray you, and authorize you fully, to solicit on my behalf that Mr. Adams may be preferred. He has always been my senior, from the commencement of my public life, and the expression of the public will being equal, this circumstance ought to give him the preference. And when so many motives will be operating to induce some of the members to change their vote, the addition of my wish may have some effect to preponderate the scale.[205]

He helped to entrench federalism in America, but the voters replaced him after his first administration for a more republican form of government. It was a very close decision.

I called on Mr. Adams on some official business. He was very seriously affected, and accosted me with these words: "Well, I understand that you are to beat me in this contest, and I will only say that I will be as faithful a subject as any you will have."

---

[205] To James Madison #2449 (M., Dec. 17, 1796.)

"Mr. Adams," said I, "this is no personal contest between you and me. Two systems of principles on the
subject of government divide our citizens into two
parties. With one of these you concur, and I with the
other. As we have been longer on the public stage
than most of those now living, our names happen to
be more generally known. One of these parties, therefore, has put your name at its head, the other mine.
Were we both to die to-day, to-morrow two other
names would be in the place of ours, without any
change in the motion of the machinery. Its motion is
from its principle, and not from you or myself."

"I believe you are right," said he, "that we are but
passive instruments, and should not suffer this
matter to affect our personal dispositions." But he did
long retain this just view of the subject. I have always
believed that the thousand calumnies which the
federalists, in bitterness of heart, and mortification at
their ejection, daily invented against me, were carried to him by their busy intriguers, and made some
impression.

Fortunate for history, the letters between Adams and you
after reconciliation, give us great insight into the founding of
the United States. This year we see the division between the
two parties as well as the division within the two parties.

Our wish is * * * that the public efforts may be
directed honestly to the public good, that peace be
cultivated, civil and religious liberty unassailed, law
and order preserved, equality of rights maintained,

and that state of property, equal or unequal, which results to every man from his own industry or that of his fathers.[206]

Should the citizens voice their desires and concerns to the President?

The right of our fellow citizens to represent to the public functionaries their opinion on proceedings interesting to them, is unquestionably a constitutional right, often useful, sometimes necessary, and will always be respectfully acknowledged by me.[207]

Presidential appointments have always been a concern to you. Not wanting individuals to lose their jobs, but also not wanting someone else's last minute appointments.

*When the public sentiment at length declared itself, and burst open the doors of honor and confidence to those whose opinions they more approved, was it to be imagined that this monopoly of office was still to be continued in the hands of the minority? Does it violate their equal rights, to assert some rights in the majority also? Is it political intolerance to claim a proportionate share in the direction of the public affairs? Can they not harmonize in society unless they have everything in their own hands? * * ***

If the will of the nation, manifested by their various elections, calls for an administration of government

---

[206] Second Inaugural Address #124 (1805)
[207] To the New Haven Committee #6878 (W., 1801.)

*according with the opinions of those elected; if, for the
fulfilment of that will, displacements are necessary,
with whom can they so justly begin as with persons
appointed in the last moments of an administration,
not for its own aid. but to begin a career at the same
time with their successors, by whom they had never
been approved, and who could scarcely expect from
them a cordial cooperation?²⁰⁸*

We have a Supreme Court nominee that has been nominated
by the Democrat President. The Republican Congress is
sitting on the consent until the new President comes in.
Congress has approved other appointments during this period.
It seems you stopped making nominations after the election
of the new President.

*In appointments to office, the government refuses to
know any difference between descriptions of republicans, all of whom are in principle, and cooperate with
the government.²⁰⁹*

*I shall make no new appointments which can be de-
ferred until the 4th of March, thinking it fair to leave
to my successor to select the agents for his own
administration.²¹⁰*

Confirmation by the Senate has been a real problem. With a
roughly fifty-fifty split in the Senate, getting a person confirmed has been difficult.

208 To the New Haven Committee #842 (W., July 1801.)
209 To William Short #6088 (M., Sep. 1808.)
210 To Dr. Logan #6044 (W., Dec. 1808.)

I have always considered the control of the Senate as meant to prevent any bias or favoritism in the President towards his own relations, his own religion, towards particular States, &c., and perhaps to keep very obnoxious persons out of offices of the first grade. But in all subordinate cases, I have ever thought that the selection made by the President ought to inspire a general confidence that it has been made on due enquiry and investigation of character, and that the Senate should interpose their negative only in those particular cases where something happens to be within their knowledge, against the character of the person, and unfitting him for the appointment.[211]

I believe the Senate goes too far in stopping presidential appointments. If the candidate gets elected by the people, they should be able to get their appointments made, unless the individual is against the government, has felonies or some serious flaw to keep them from being approved, like not being able to get a Top Secret clearance rating. The political appointee should not be turned down based on his convictions and beliefs, that is why the President appointed them. The same goes for Governors and appointments on the state level.

To exhibit recommendations would be to turn the Senate into a court of honor, or a court of slander, and to expose the character of every man nominated to an ordeal, without his own consent, subjecting the Senate to heats and waste of time.[212]

---

[211] To Albert Gallatin #6082 (1803.)
[212] To Albert Gallatin #6168 (1803.)

To you I need not make the observation that of all the duties imposed on the executive head of a government, appointment to office is the most difficult and irksome.[213]

Patronage was always a concern of yours.

Let us deserve well of our country by making her interests the end of all our plans, and not our own pomp, patronage and irresponsibility.[214]

The republicans complain that the influence and patronage of the Executive are to become so great as to govern the Legislature.[215]

The cost is tremendous to the taxpayers as the bureaucracy continues to grow and it does overshadow the Legislature.

The multiplication of public offices, increase of expense beyond income, growth and entailment of a public debt, are indications soliciting the employment of the pruning knife.[216]

Our Nation's leaders say that it is hard to cut the size of our government. Would a President Donald Trump or a President Hillary Clinton wield the pruning knife? What happened in the second revolution when you became President?

Among those [officers] who are dependent on Executive discretion, I have begun the reduction of what

---

[213] To George Clinton #6076 (W., May 1801.)
[214] To Albert Gallatin #8521 (W., 1802.)
[215] To Thomas Pinckney #1530 (Pa., 1792.)
[216] To Spencer Roane # 6112 (M., 1821.)

was deemed necessary. The expense of diplomatic agency have been considerably diminished. The Inspectors of internal revenue, who were found to obstruct the accountability of the institution, have been discontinued.

It appears that the Internal Revenue has again been accused and found to be obstructing the institution. The IRS has obstructed conservative non-profits from getting tax exempt status; while at the same time paying billions in tax refunds to illegal immigrants and millions to prisoners filing false claims. It is time to change our tax structure, to simplify it.

Several agencies created by Executive authority, on salaries fixed by that also, have been suppressed, and should suggest the expediency of regulating that by law, so as to subject its exercises to legislative inspection and sanction. Other reformations of the same kind will be pursued with that caution which is requisite in removing useless things, not to injure what is retained. But the great mass of public offices is established by law, and, therefore, by law alone can be abolished.[217]

Did Congress assist in the pruning by changing the laws establishing programs?

*The session of the first Congress, convened since republicanism has recovered its ascendancy, * * * will pretty completely fulfil all the desires of the people. They have reduced the army and navy to what is*

---

[217] First Annual Message #6170 (Dec. 1801.)

barely necessary. They are disarming executive pat-ronage and preponderance, by putting down one-half the offices of the United States, which are no longer necessary. These economies have enabled them to suppress all the internal taxes, and still to make such provision for the payment of their public debt as to discharge that in eighteen years. They have lopped off a parasite limb, planted by their predecessors on their judiciary for party purposes, and they are opening the doors of hospitality to the fugitives from the op-pressions of other countries.[218]

So you cut the size of government in half?

We have put down the great mass of offices which gave such patronage to the President. These had been so numerous, that presenting themselves to the public eye at all times and places, office began to be looked to as a resource for every man whose affairs were getting into derangement, or who was too indolent to pursue his profession, and for young men just enter-ing into life. In short, it was poisoning the very source of industry, by presenting an easier resource for a livelihood, and was corrupting the principles of the great mass of those who passed a wishful eye on office.[219]

Why is the Federal Government so big when the Constitution gives them so little to do?

---

[218] To General Kosciusko #1582 (W., April 1802.)
[219] To Thomas McKean #6063 (W., Feb. 1803.)

When we consider that this government is charged with the eternal and mutual relations only of these States; that the States themselves have principal care of our persons, our property, and our reputation, constituting the great field of human concerns, we may well doubt whether our organization is not too complicated, too expensive; whether offices and officers have not been multiplied unnecessarily, and sometimes injuriously to the service they were meant to promote. I will cause to be laid before you an essay towards a statement of those who, under public employment of various kinds, draw money from the treasury or from our citizens.[220]

Another thing you tried to do is hire local. You did not hire a New Englander for a position in South Carolina.

Where an office is local we never go out of the limits for the officer.[221]

I do hope the incoming President and Congress takes notice as to what may be done.

Our predecessors, in order to increase expense, debt, taxation, and patronage, tried always how much they could give.[222]

So they expanded the size of government and patronage.

---

[220] First Annual Message #6171 (Dec. 1801.)
[221] To Caeser A. Rodney #6103 (W., 1806.)
[222] To James Monroe #2850 (W., 1803.)

Have you considered all the consequences of your proposition respecting post roads? I view it as a source of boundless patronage to the Executive, jobbing to members of Congress and their friends, and a bottomless abyss of public money. You will begin by appropriating only the surplus of the Post Office revenues; but the other revenues will soon be called into their aid, and it will be the source of eternal scramble among the members, who can get the most money wasted in their State; and they will always get most who are meanest.

Congressmen still fight for spending in their districts. It is like Congressmen fighting for military bases, for bridges to nowhere and roads, or for some contractor in their state. The Army gets more tanks even though they do not want them. It doesn't matter that they are not wanted as long as the influential Congressmen gets the spending in his district. The squeaky wheel gets the grease.

We have thought, hitherto, that the roads of a State could not be so well administered even by the State Legislature, as by the magistracy of the county, on the spot. How will it be when a member of New Hampshire is to mark out a road for Georgia? Does the power to establish post roads, given you by the Constitution, mean that you shall make the roads, or only select from those already made, those on which there shall be a post? If the term be equivocal (and I really do not think it so,) which is the safer construction? That which permits a majority of Congress to go cutting down mountains and bridging of rivers, or the other, which, if too restricted, may be referred to the States for amendment, securing still due measure and proportion among us, and providing some means of information to the members of Congress tantamount to that ocular inspection, which, even in our county determinations, the magistrate finds cannot be supplied by any other evidence?

Now there is federal matching funds on most roads in America. The interstate system was set up for national defense.

The fortification of harbors was liable to great objection. But national circumstances furnished some color. In this case there is none. The roads of America are the best in the world except those of France and England. But does the state of our population, the extent of our internal commerce, the want of sea and river navigation, call for such expense on roads here, or are our means adequate to it?[223]

The Federal Government is also into ports. I recall President Clinton wanting to give the management of some American ports to the Communist China and to Saudi Arabia. I wonder how much money went to him for his speaking engagements and the Clinton Foundation?

When you took over as President, what did you do about the appointees already in place?

I have never removed a man merely because he was a federalist. I have never wished them to give a vote

---

[223] To James Madison #6807 (M., March 1796.)

at an election, but according to their own wishes. But as no government could discharge its duties to the best advantage of its citizens, if its agents were in a regular course of thwarting instead of executing all its measures, and were employing the patronage and influence of their offices against the government and its measures, I have only requested they would be quiet, and they should be safe; that if their conscience urges them to take an active and zealous part in opposition, it ought also to urge them to retire from a post which they could not conscientiously conduct with fidelity to the trust reposed in them; and on failure to retire, I have removed them; that is to say, those who maintained an active and zealous opposition to the government.[224]

I can see replacing those openly and actively opposed to the administration. It must be hard to get the best qualified to make appointments.

I am thankful at all times for information on the subject of appointments, even when it comes too late to be used. It is more difficult and more painful than all the other duties of my office, and one in which I am sufficiently conscious that in voluntary error must often be committed.[225]

In a government like ours it is necessary to embrace in its administration as great a mass of confidence as possible, by employing those who have a character

---

[224] To John Page #6161 (W., July 1807.)
[225] To Joseph B. Varnum #6042 (W.,1807.)

with the public, of their own, and not merely a secondary one through the Executive.[226] *No man will ever bring out of the presidency the reputation which carries him into it.*[227]

Well that's good, because the only way the character of our current candidates for President can go, is up. The United States is in a position now where one of our parties candidates, Donald Trump, a political outsider, has good issues but no tact, so the media goes after the one blurb and skips the real message; and the other, Hillary Clinton, former First Lady, was under active investigation by the FBI, for her actions as Secretary of State in transmitting classified intelligence and providing "materially false" information during the investigation. Her husband, former President Bill Clinton, was the second president in history to be impeached. The IRS is investigating the Clinton Foundation for a "pay to play scheme." Sixty-four Congressmen also asked the FBI and the Federal Trade Commission to examine the Clinton foundation alleging criminal conduct. The current President Barack Obama has endorsed Hillary Clinton and the Democrat National Committee, through their convention process has made her the Democrat presidential candidate.

I sincerely wish we could see our government so secured as to depend less on the character of the person in whose hands it is trusted.[228]

---

[226] The Anas #112 (April, 1806.)
[227] To Edward Rutledge #6913 (M., 1796.)
[228] To Moses Robinson #6898 (W., March 1801.)

What a state of affairs we are in, the President of the United States endorsing someone whose character is so questioned, and the Democrats in America voting for her.

There are two classes of disputants most frequently to be met with among us. The first is of young students, just entered the threshold of science, with a first view of its outlines, not yet filled up with the details and modifications which a further progress would bring to their knowledge.

The other consists of the ill tempered and rude men in society, who have taken up a passion for politics. From both of these classes of disputants, * * * keep aloof, as you would from the infected subjects of yellow fever or pestilence. Consider yourself, when with them, as among the patients of Bedlam, needing medical more than moral counsel. Be a listener only, keep within yourself, and endeavor to establish with yourself the habit of silence, especially on politics.

In the fevered state of our country, no good can ever result from any attempt to set one of these fiery zealots to rights, either in fact or principle. They are determined as to the facts they will believe, and the opinions on which they will act. Get by them, therefore, as you would by an angry bull; it is not for a man of sense to dispute the road with such an animal. You will be more exposed than others to have these animals shaking their horns at you, because of the relation in which you stand with me.

Full of political venom, and willing to see me and to hate me as a chief in the antagonistic party, your presence will be to them what the vomit grass is to the sick dog, a nostrum for producing ejaculation. Look upon them exactly with that eye, and pity them as objects to whom you can administer only occasional ease.

My character is not within their power. It is in the hands of my fellow citizens at large, and will be consigned to honor or infamy by the verdict of the republican mass of our country, according to what themselves will have seen, not what their enemies and mine shall have said. Never, therefore, consider these puppies in politics as requiring any notice from you, and always show that you are not afraid to leave my character to the umpirage of public opinion.[229]

Donald Trump and Bernie Sanders come to mind, Mr. Jefferson. Donald Trump, the Republican candidate, some consider the ill-tempered and rude man, who many think will hopefully get our nation back on track. People like him for what he says, and people dislike him for the same reason. He is new on the scene, some question if he will stick to his word. Others fear the lack of tact with those around the world. All of it is refreshing as compared to the opposition.

We have no rose without its thorn; no pleasure without alloy. It is the law of our existence; and we must acquiesce. It is the condition annexed to all our

---

[229] To Thomas Jefferson Randolph #2243 (W., 1808.)

pleasures, not by us who receive, but by Him who gives them.[230]

I believe he is the heart of the United States right now. You said America needs a revolution now and then, and he is our revolution.

It can never be too often repeated that the time for fixing every essential right, on a legal basis, is while our rulers are honest and ourselves united.[231]

The other, Bernie Sanders, a Democrat and socialist, who has the young people following, because of the promise of free college and the wiping out of student loans.

Aware of the tendency of power to degenerate into abuse, the worthies of our own country have secured its independence by the establishment of a Constitution and form of government for our nation, calculated to prevent as well as to correct abuse.[232] *The information of the people at large can alone make them the safe, as they are the sole depositary of our political and religious freedom.*[233]

*I dislike strongly [in the new Constitution] the perpetual reeligibility of the President. This, I fear, will make that an office for life, first, and then hereditary. * * * However, I shall hope that before there is danger of this change taking place in the office of*

230 To Mrs. Cosway #6307 (P., 1786.)
231 Notes on Virginia #7206 (1782.)
232 To Tammany Society of Washington #15 (1809.)
233 To William Duane #2418 (M., 1810.)

President, the good sense and free spirit of our countrymen will make the changes necessary to prevent it.[234]

Fortunately that was taken care of after Franklin Roosevelt was elected four times. It is the 22nd Amendment, ratified in 1951, limiting the President to two terms. Franklin Roosevelt was the only President to break the two term maximum tradition. But as you can see, some continue to want it as a dynasty, as the Clintons, Bushes and Kennedys tried to do in recent years.

The transaction of business with foreign nations is Executive altogether. It belongs, then, to the head of that department, except as to such portions of it as are specially submitted to the Senate. Exceptions are to be construed strictly.[235]

What do you think about President Obama again recognizing Cuba, after it became a communist country in 1959 and relations were severed in 1961?

I candidly confess, that I have ever looked on Cuba as the most interesting addition which could ever be made to our system of States. The control which, with Florida Point, this island would give us over the Gulf of Mexico, and the countries an isthmus bordering on it, as well as all those whose waters flow into it, would fill up the measure of our political well-being.[236]

---

[234] To General Washington #6883 (P., 1788.)
[235] Opinion on the Powers of the Senate #6889 (1790.)
[236] To President Monroe #1947 (M., 1823.)

It is very unfortunate Mr. Jefferson, that we must endure the out and out lies that officials in our government tell us. And when the individuals are caught, the media continues covering up for the individuals. A good example is former Secretary of State Hillary Clinton on the Benghazi scandal, with Americans being killed, and a filmmaker being blamed by the administration. The reports have come out showing her lies, but the media says no big deal.

It is of great importance to set a resolution, not to be shaken, never to tell an untruth. There is no vice so mean, so pitiful, so contemptible; and he who permits himself to tell a lie once, finds it much easier to do it a second and a third time, till at length it becomes habitual; he tells lies without attending to it, and truths without the world's believing him. This falsehood of the tongue leads to that of the heart, and in time depraves all its good dispositions.[237]

Well, I think it is habitual with Mrs. Clinton. Just ask her about her emails and in home server. The FBI stated that she did in fact lie to the American people, but she doesn't need to be held accountable, as she did not intend to violate the law. Unfortunately, the FBI must not have watched her town hall meetings where she laughed and bragged about it. When questioning Hillary Clinton, the FBI did not administer a sworn oath and did not record the interview. Who is running the country. Do we not have a Congress that will say enough already?

---

[237] To Peter Carr #8604 (P., 1785.)

The firmness with which the people have with stood the late abuses of the press, the discernment they have manifested between truth and falsehood, show that they may safely be trusted to hear everything true and false, and to form a correct judgment between them.[238]

I hope you are correct and there is time for the citizens to understand. As we discussed, we are in a heated election, with the country divided by the political parties.

It is not wisdom alone, but public confidence in that wisdom, which can support an administration.[239]

If we are faithful to our country, if we acquiesce, with good will, in the decisions of the majority, and the nation moves in mass in the same direction, although it may not be that which every individual thinks best, we have nothing to fear from any quarter.[240]

Not in our day, but at no distant one, we may shake a rod over the heads of all, which may make the stoutest of them tremble. But I hope our wisdom will grow with our power, and teach us, that the less we use our power, the greater will it be.[241]

---

[238] To Judge Tyler #8600 (W.,1804.)
[239] To President Monroe #7106 (M., 1824.)
[240] To Virginia Baptists #4948 (1808.)
[241] To Thomas Leiper #8708 (M., 1815.)

We are in that position now. One of my concerns Mr. Jefferson is what is happening within our country, the arming of many of the federal employees. It is looking like a police state.

Our citizens may be deceived for awhile, and have been deceived; but as long as the presses can be protected, we may trust to them for light.[242]

The people of every country are the only safe guardians of their own rights, and are the only instruments which can be used for their destruction. And certainly they would never consent to be so used were they not deceived. To avoid this they should be instructed to a certain degree.[243]

Mr. Jefferson, I think we are instructing them to a certain degree here. There are more than 200,000 Federal Government officers, not in the Department of Defense, carrying firearms and have arrest authority. We have more of them than we have Marines. Makes me wonder what President Obama is up to, especially with his Martial Law Executive Order for peace times. He wants to take the arms from the citizens as he armed up. The military is not even allowed to be armed on a military base. We are talking like IRS agents, Bureau of Land Management, postal inspectors, the Food & Drug Administration and Small Business Administration to name a few of the agencies.

A government of reason is better than one of force.[244]

---

[242] To Archibald Stuart #6569 (M., 1799.)
[243] To John Wyche #6618 (M., 1809.)
[244] To Richard Rush #7169 (M., 1820.)

Lay down true principles and adhere to them inflexibly. Do not be frightened into their surrender by the alarms of the timid, or the croakings of wealth against the ascendency of the people. If experience be called for, appeal to that of our fifteen or twenty governments for forty years, and show me where the people have done half the mischief in these forty years, that a single despot would have done in a single year.[245]

The spirit of 1776 is not dead. It has only been slumbering. The body of the American people is substantially republican. But their virtuous feelings have been played on by some fact with more fiction; they have been the dupes of artful manoeuvres, and made for a moment to be willing instruments in forging chains for themselves. But time and truth. have dissipated the delusion, and opened their eyes.[246]

*To constrain the brute force of the people, * * * governments deem it necessary to keep them down by hard labor, poverty and ignorance, and to take from them, as from bees, so much of their earnings, as that unremitting labor shall be necessary to obtain a sufficient surplus barely to sustain a scanty and miserable life. And these earnings they apply to maintain their privileged orders in splendor and idleness, to fascinate the eyes of the people, and excite in them an*

---

[245] To Samuel Kerchival #6657 (M., 1816.)
[246] To T. Lomax #6568 (M., March 1799.)

humble adoration and submission, as to an order of superior beings.[247]

The President may issue pardons. Both Democrat and Republicans have issued many in recent years. President Clinton's seemed to be abusive, including pardoning his brother. He spent his last day in office issuing pardons very similar to President Adams spending his last day appointing judges.

In every government on earth is some trace of human weakness, some germ of corruption and degeneracy, which cunning will discover, and wickedness insensibly open, cultivate and improve.[248]

Part of the 450 individuals pardoned by President Clinton included 16 members of a Puerto Rican group that had set off 120 bombs in the United States. He also pardoned Mark Rich, who owed $48 million in taxes, and had many counts of fraud. Riches wife gave Hillary Clinton campaign contributions and donated to the Clinton Library. Hillary's brothers were also investigated for receiving hundreds of thousands of dollars in what appeared to be a "quid pro quo," pay to play scheme. Some of the money was paid back to those receiving the pardons.

Where the law of the majority ceases to be acknowledged, there government ends; the law of the strongest takes its place, and life and property are his who can take them.[249]

---

247 To William Johnson #6605 (M., 1823.)
248 Notes on Virginia #3491 (1782.)
249 To Annapolis Citizens #4937 (1809.)

Besides the apparent fraud with some of our nation's leaders, we, by the size of our jails and prisons, have a considerable number of people stealing in this country.

A right to property is founded in our natural wants, in the means with which we are endowed to satisfy these wants, and the right to what we acquire by those means without violating the similar rights of other sensible beings.[250]

I have made it a rule to grant no pardon in any criminal case but on the recommendation of the judges who sat on the trial, and the district attorney, or two of them. I believe it a sound rule, and not to be departed from but in extraordinary cases.[251] *It would be against every rule of prudence for me to undertake to revise the verdict of a jury on ex parte affidavits and recommendations.*[252]

The power of pardon, committed to Executive discretion, [can] never be more properly exercised than where citizens [are] suffering without the authority of law, or, which [is] equivalent, under a law unauthorized by the Constitution, and therefore null.[253]

Anything else you would like to say to the President and the presidential candidates?

---

[250] To Dupont de Nemours #7056 (P.F., 1816.)
[251] To Albert Gallatin #6389 (M., 1806.)
[252] To George Blake #6392 (W., 1808.)
[253] To Spenser Roane #6393 (P.F., 1819.)

The just standing of all nations is the health and security of all.[254]

I shall need the favor of that Being in whose hands we are, Who led our forefathers, as Israel of old, from their native land, and planted them in a country flowing with all the necessaries and comforts of life; Who has covered our infancy with His providence, and our riper years with His wisdom and power; and to whose goodness I ask you to join with me in supplications, that He will so enlighten the minds of your servants, guide their councils, and prosper their measures, that whatsoever they do shall result in your good, and shall secure to you the peace, friendship, and approbation of all nations.[255]

Amen, Mr. Jefferson.

---

[254] To James Maury #5660 (M., 1812.)
[255] Second Inaugural Address #2161 (1805.)

ON THE SUPREME COURT

At the establishment of our Constitutions, the judiciary bodies were supposed to be the most helpless and harmless members of the government. Experience, however, soon showed in what way they were to become the most dangerous; that the insufficiency of the means provided for their removal gave them a freehold and irresponsibility in office; that their decisions, seeming to concern individual suitors only, pass silent and unheeded by the public at large; that these decisions, nevertheless, become law by precedent, sapping, by little and little, the foundations of the Constitution, and working its change by construction, before any one has perceived that that invisible and helpless worm has been busily employed in consuming its substance. In truth, man is not made to be trusted for life, if secured against all liability to account[256]

---

[256] To A. Coray #4184 (M., 1823.)

My, my Mr. Jefferson. Why don't you please tell us what you really feel? It definitely sounds like there is mistrust.

*The Judiciary of the United States is the subtle corps of sappers and miners constantly working under ground to undermine the foundations of our confederated fabric. They are construing our Constitution from a coordination of a general and special government to a general and supreme one alone. This will lay all things at their feet, and they are too well versed in English law to forget the maxim, "boni judicis est ampliare jurisdictionem" [good justice is broad jurisdiction]. * * **

Having found from experience, that impeachment is an impracticable thing, a mere scare-crow, they consider themselves secure for life; they skulk from responsibility to public opinion, the only remaining hold on them, under a practice first introduced into England by Lord Mansfield. An opinion is huddled up in conclave, perhaps by a majority of one, delivered as if unanimous, and with the silent acquiescence of lazy or timid associates, by a crafty chief judge, who sophisticates the law to his mind, by the turn of his own reasoning.

A judiciary law was once reported by the Attorney General to Congress, requiring each judge to deliver his opinion seriatim and openly, and then to give it in writing to the clerk to be entered in the record. A judiciary independent of a king or executive alone, is a good thing; but independence of the will of the nation is a solecism, at least in a republican govern-ment.[257]

Supreme Court Justice Clarence Thomas has written that the Court has a troubling tendency "to bend the rules when any effort to limit abortion, or even to speak in opposition to abortion, is at issue. * * * Our law is now so riddled with special exceptions for special rights that our decisions deliver neither predictability nor the promise of a judiciary bound by the rule of law. * * * "[C]ourts are not roving commissions assigned to pass judgment on the validity of the Nation's laws." * * * But the problem now goes beyond that. If our recent cases illustrate anything, it is how easily the Court tinkers with levels of scrutiny to achieve its desired result.

The Court has simultaneously transformed judicially created rights, like the right to abortion, into preferred constitutional rights, while disfavoring many of the rights actually enumerated in the Constitution, But our Constitution renounces the notion that some constitutional rights are more equal than others. A law either infringes a constitutional right, or not; there is no room for the judiciary to invent tolerable degrees of encroachment. Unless the Court abides by one set of rules to adjudicate constitutional rights, it will continue reducing constitutional law to policy-driven value judgments until the last shreds of its legitimacy disappear. * * * The majority's embrace of a jurisprudence of rights-specific exceptions and balancing tests is "a regrettable concession of defeat—an acknowledgement that we have passed the point where 'law,'

---

[257] To Thomas Ritchie #4186 (M., 1820.)

properly speaking, has any further application.""""[258]

I must comfort myself with the hope that the judges will see the importance and the duty of giving their country the only evidence they can give of fidelity to its Constitution and integrity in the administration of its laws; that is to say, by every one's giving his opinion seriatim and publicly on the cases he decides. Let him prove by his reasoning that he has read the papers, that he has considered the case, that in the application of the law to it, he uses his own judgment independently and unbiased by party views and personal favor or disfavor.

Throw himself in every case on God and his country; both will excuse him for error and value him for his honesty. The very idea of cooking up opinions in conclave, begets suspicions that something passes which fears the public ear, and this, spreading by degrees, must produce at some time abridgment of tenure, facility of removal, or some other modification which may promise a remedy. For, in truth, there is at this time more hostility to the Federal Judiciary than to any other organ of the government.[259]

Do not comfort yourself too much Mr. Jefferson. The Courts do not recognize "God and country," and they credit you with taking God out of the country.

Justice Clarence Thomas No. 15–274. Argued March 2, 2016—Decided June 27, 2016 https://www.supremecourt.gov/opinions/15pdf/15-274_p8k0.pdf
259 To William Johnson #8226 (M., 1823.)

If, indeed, a judge goes against law so grossly, so pal-pably, as no imputable degree of folly can account for, and nothing but corruption, malice or wilful wrong can explain, and especially if circumstances prove such motives, he may be punished for the cor-ruption, the malice, the wilful wrong; but not for the error.[260]

I wish that was the case, unfortunately court judges get their way. When questions of the authority of the Supreme Court comes from a Supreme Court justice, it makes you stop and think, that even some of the justices have the same concerns as you.

The question whether the judges are invested with exclusive authority to decide on the constitutionality of a law, has been heretofore a subject of considera-tion with me in the exercise of official duties. Certain-ly there is not a word in the Constitution which has given that power to them more than to the Executive or Legislative branches. Questions of property, of character and of crime being ascribed to the judges, through a definite course of legal proceeding, laws involving such questions belong, of course, to them; and as they decide on them ultimately and without appeal, they of course decide for themselves.

The constitutional validity of the law or laws again prescribing Executive action, and to be administered by that branch ultimately and without appeal, the Executive must decide for themselves also, whether,

---

[260] The Batture Case #2736 (1812.)

under the Constitution, they are valid or not. So also as to laws governing the proceedings of the Legislature, that body must judge for itself the constitutionality of the law, and equally without appeal or control from its coordinate branches. And, in general, that branch which is to act ultimately, and without appeal, on any law, is the rightful expositor of the validity of the law, uncontrolled by the opinions of the other coordinate authorities.[261]

*It is a very dangerous doctrine to consider the judges as the ultimate arbiters of all constitutional questions. It is one which would place us under the despotism of an oligarchy. * * * The Constitution has erected no such single tribunal, knowing that to whatever hands confided, with the corruptions of time and party, its members would become despots. It has more wisely made all the departments coequal and cosovereign within themselves.*[262]

Can you give me an example of what you are talking about?

If the Legislature fails to pass laws for a census, for paying the Judges and other officers of government, for establishing a militia, for naturalization as prescribed by the Constitution, or if they fail to meet in Congress, the Judges cannot issue their mandamus to them; if the President fails to supply the place of a judge, to appoint other civil or military officers, to issue requisite commissions, the Judges cannot force

---

[261] To W. H. Torrance #4486 (M., 1815.)
[262] To William C. Jarvis #8228 (M., 1820.)

him. They can issue their mandamus or distringas to no executive or legislative officer to enforce the fulfilment of their official duties any more than the President or Legislature may issue orders to the Judges or their officers. Betrayed by English example, and unaware, as it should seem, of the control of our Constitution in this particular, they have at times overstepped their limit by undertaking to command executive officers in the discharge of their executive duties; but the Constitution, in keeping the three departments distinct and independent restrains the authority of the Judges to judiciary organs, as it does the Executive and Legislative to executive and legislative organs.

The Judges certainly have more frequent occasion to act on constitutional questions, because the laws of meum and tuum and of criminal action, forming the great mass of the system of law, constitute their particular department. When the legislative or executive functionaries act unconstitutionally, they are responsible to the people in their elective capacity. The exemption of the Judges from that is quite dangerous enough.[263]

The principle of the Constitution is that of a separation of Legislative, Executive and Judiciary functions, except in cases specified. If this principle be not expressed in direct terms, it is clearly the spirit of the

---

[263] To William C. Jarvis #8229 (M., 1820.)

Constitution, and it ought to be so commented and acted on by every friend of free government.[264]

I believe lifetime appointments to be a major problem of the judicial system. When you have a swing in the Presidency and or in Congress to constitutional conservatism, you still have the liberal judiciary overruling issues, or the opposite. We have recently had several states, that have had laws and constitutional amendments overturned by the federal judiciary on issues that the Constitution designated to the states.

The revolution of 1800 was as real a revolution in the principles of our government as that of 1776 was in its form; not effected, indeed, by the sword, as that, but by the rational and peaceable instrument of reform, the suffrage of the people. The nation declared its will by dismissing functionaries of one principle, and electing those of another, in the two branches, Executive and Legislative, submitted to their election. Over the Judiciary department, the Constitution had deprived them of their control. That, therefore, has continued the reprobated system, and although new matter has been occasionally incorporated into the old, yet the leaven of the old mass seems to assimilate to itself the new, and after twenty years confirmation of the federal system by the voice of the nation, declared through the medium of elections, we find the Judiciary on every occasion, still driving us into consolidation.[265]

---

[264] To James Madison #6851 (M., Jan. 1797.)
[265] To Spencer Roane #7340 (P.F., 1819.)

So you had the political change of the President and Congress when you were elected, but still had the federalist judges.

They have retired into the judiciary as a stronghold. There the remains of federalism are to be preserved and fed from the treasury, and from that battery all the works of republicanism are to be beaten down and erased. By a fraudulent use of the Constitution, which has made judges irremovable, they have multiplied useless judges merely to strengthen their phalanx.[266]

It is so hard to impeach a judge.

In the General Government in this instance, we have gone even beyond the English caution, by requiring a vote of two-thirds, in one of the Houses, for removing a Judge; a vote so impossible, where any defence is made, before men of ordinary prejudices and passions, that our Judges are effectually independent of the nation. But this ought not to be.[267]

What would you recommend?

* * * that of appointing for a term of years only, with a capacity of reappointment if their conduct has been approved.[268]

Sum it up for us Mr. Jefferson. It appears the Judicial Branch has been out of control for the last couple hundred years, but

---

[266] To John Dickinson #2961 (W., 1801.)
[267] Autobiography #3857 (1821.)
[268] To M. Coray #3858 (M.,1823.)

I think it is much worse now. There is no rhyme or reason to the courts actions now according to Justice Thomas.

The great object of my fear is the Federal Judiciary. That body, like gravity, ever acting, with noiseless foot, and unalarming advance, gaining ground step by step, and holding what it gains, is engulfing insidiously the special governments into the jaws of that which feeds them.[269]

We already see the power, installed for life, responsible to no authority (for impeachment is not even a scare-crow), advancing with a noiseless and steady pace to the great object of consolidation. The foundations are already deeply laid by their decisions for the annihilation of constitutional State rights, and the removal of every check, every counterpoise to the engulfing power of which themselves are to make a sovereign part. If ever this vast country is brought under a single government, it will be one of the most extensive corruption, indifferent and incapable of a wholesome care over so wide a spread of surface. This will not be borne, and you will have to choose between reformation and revolution. If I know the spirit of this country, the one or the other is inevitable. Before the canker is become inveterate, before its venom has reached so much of the body politic as to get beyond control, remedy should be applied.[270]

What do you suggest be done to save our nation?

[269] To Spenser Roane #8221 (M.,1821.)
[270] To William T. Barry #1171 (M., 1822.)

*** to check these unconstitutional invasions of State rights by the Federal judiciary. How? Not by impeachment, in the first instance, but by a strong protestation of both houses of Congress that such and such doctrines, advanced by the Supreme Court, are contrary to the Constitution; and if afterwards they relapse into the same heresies, impeach and set the whole adrift. For what was the government divided into three branches, but that each should watch over the others and oppose their usurpations?[271]*

We have a weak Congress, afraid of attacking anything the Supreme Court or the President does. Do we need to elect a new forceful Congress or educate them to what their duties are and who they are working for?

*The Legislative and Executive branches may sometimes err, but elections and dependence will bring them to rights. The Judiciary branch is the instrument which, working like gravity, without intermission, is to press us at last into one consolidated mass. *** If Congress fails to shield the States from dangers so palpable and so imminent, the States must shield themselves, and meet the invader foot to foot.[272]*

The States are being run roughshod by the Supreme Court, ruling against their constitutional amendments voted on by the majority of their citizens. If the Congress does not act after this election, then the States should call a convention for proposing amendments.

---

[271] To Nathaniel Macon #8236 (M., Aug. 1821.)
[272] To Archibald Thweat #8237 (M., 1821.)

ON THE ECONOMY

There is not a country on earth where there is great-er tranquillity; where the laws are milder, or better obeyed; where every one is more attentive to his own business or meddles less with that of others; where strangers are better received, more hospitably treat-ed, and with a more sacred respect.[273]

A rising nation, spread over a wide and fruitful land, traversing all the seas with the rich productions of their industry, engaged in commerce with nations who feel power and forget right, advancing rapidly to destinies beyond the reach of mortal eye, when I contemplate these transcendent objects, and see the honor, the happiness, and the hopes of this beloved country committed to the issue and the auspices of

---

[273] To Mrs. Cosway #8715 (P., 1786.)

this day, I shrink from the contemplation, and humble myself before the magnitude of the undertaking.[274]

I sincerely wish that the whole Union may accommodate their interests to each other, and play into their hands mutually as members of the same family, that the wealth and strength of any one part should be viewed as the wealth and strength of the whole.[275]

It sounds so idyllic Mr. Jefferson, but looking at the other nations, I guess I would tend to agree with you.

There is not a nation under the sun enjoying more present prosperity, nor with more in prospect.[276]

But as you are aware, whenever you have more than one person involved with something, there are problems. Much of the United States' economic problems are rooted with the Federal Government.

In so complicated a science as political economy, no one axiom can be laid down as wise and expedient for all times and circumstances, and for their contraries.[277]

We have had a problem of the Federal Government interfering with state issues. States are threatened with the withholding of Federal money if the States do not do what is demanded by the Federal Government. This has happened many times under the Obama administration, whether it be

---

[274] First Inaugural Address #8693 (1801.)
[275] To Hugh Williamson #8667 (Pa., Feb. 1798.)
[276] To C. W. F. Dumas #7070 (Pa., 1791.)
[277] To Benjamin Austin #2365 (M., Jan. 1816.)

regarding the use of coal, or the bathrooms that we use.

Warring against the principles of the great body of the American people, the delusion of the people is necessary to the dominant party. I see the extent to which that delusion has been already carried, and I see there is no length to which it may not be pushed by a party in possession of the revenues and the legal authorities of the United States, for a short time, indeed, but yet long enough to admit much particular mischief. There is no event, therefore, however atrocious, which may not be expected.[278]

What institution is insusceptible of abuse in wicked hands?[279] Agriculture, manufactures, commerce and navigation, the four pillars of our prosperity, are the most thriving when left most free to individual enterprise. Protection from casual embarrassments, however, may sometimes be seasonably interposed.[280]

You did not mention Wall Street. Presidential candidate Hillary Clinton has received much of her campaign donations as well as income from there.

*The capital employed in paper speculation * * * nourishes in our citizens habits of vice and idleness, instead of industry and morality.[281]*

---

278 To Samuel Smith #2172 (M., 1798.)
279 To L. H. Girardin #20 (M., 1815.)
280 First Annual Message #216 (Dec. 1801.)
281 To President Washington #1129 (Pa., 1792.)

Money, and not morality, is the principle of commercial nations.[282] *Every discovery which multiplies the subsistence of man must be a matter of joy to every friend of humanity.*[283]

We continue to have discoveries which change our lives. Many people living went from horse and buggies as transportation, to seeing space travel. In agricultural terms you will understand, it is from planting one row of corn at a time, to forty eight rows at a time.

*The construction applied by the General Government (as is evidenced by sundry of their proceedings) to those parts of the Constitution of the United States which delegate to Congress a power "to lay and collect taxes, duties, imposts, and excises, to pay the debts and provide for the common defence and general welfare of the United States" and "to make all laws which shall be necessary and proper for carrying into execution the powers vested by the Constitution in the government of the United States, or in any department or officer thereof", goes to the destruction of all limits prescribed to their power by the Constitution. * * * Words meant by the instrument to be subsidiary only to the execution of limited powers, ought not to be so construed as themselves to give unlimited powers, nor a part to be so taken as to destroy the whole residue of that instrument.*[284]

---

[282] To John Taylor #5384 (1810.)
[283] To Monsieur L' Hommande #8199 (P., 1787.)
[284] Kentucky Resolutions #3393 (1798.)

Congress continues to spend without reservation as if the people's money has no limit. Party affiliation does not matter.

We are ruined if we do not overrule the principles that "the more we owe, the more prosperous we shall be"; "that a public debt furnishes the means of enterprise"; "that if ours should be once paid off, we should incur another by any means however extravagant."[285]

One of the biggest and most expensive fiascos in recent years is Obamacare. Congress approved a bill they had not read, that had far reaching implications. They had no constitutional authority to do it based on your definition of the "general welfare clause". It had been an issue pushed by President Obama and the legislative leadership. It was a bad plan that was forced on to private industry and the citizens of this nation. Speaker Pelosi bragged that Congress would have plenty of time to read it after the bill was passed. Now the people and the government are tied in a plan that is not working for the people and their medical care, nor for the doctors and hospitals. The cost is huge and all the people are still not covered.

To lay taxes to provide for the general welfare of the United States, that is to say, "to lay taxes for the purpose of providing for the general welfare". For the laying of taxes is the power, and the general welfare the purpose for which the power is to be exercised. They are not to lay taxes ad libitum for any purpose they please; but only to pay the debts or provide for the welfare of the Union. In like manner, they are not to do anything they please to provide for the general

---

[285] To James Monroe #2068 (Pa., 1791.)

welfare, but only <u>to lay taxes</u> for that purpose. To consider the latter phrase, not as describing the purpose of the first, but as giving a distinct and independent power to do any act they please, which might be for the good of the Union, would render all the preceding and subsequent enumerations of power completely useless.

It would reduce the whole instrument to a single phrase, that of instituting a Congress with power to do whatever would be for the good of the United States; and as they would be the sole judges of the good or evil, it would be also a power to do whatever evil they please. It is an established rule of construction where a phrase will bear either of two meanings, to give it that which will allow some meaning to the other parts of the instrument, and not that which would render all the others useless. Certainly no such universal power was meant to be given them. It was intended to lace them up strictly within the enumerated powers, and those without which, as means, these powers could not be carried into effect.[286]

Various groups, businesses and industries continue to lobby Congress for interventions to help their business interests.

I told President Washington there was great difference between the little accidental schemes of self-interest, which would take place in every body of

---

[286] To George Washington, LOC February 15, 1791, http://hdl.loc.gov/loc.mss/mtj.mtjbib005219

men, and influence their votes, and a regular system for forming a corps of interested persons.[287] *And with grief and shame it must be acknowledged that his machine was not without effect; that even in this, the birth of our government, some members were found sordid enough to bend their duty to their interests, and to look after personal rather than public good.*[288]

It is not any better now, Mr. Jefferson. President Obama, when campaigning for office, said he would put the coal industry out of business. Other energy businesses have been subsidized such as wind and solar power to do it. Organizations and lobbyists have spent millions of dollars promoting their concerns. I believe you called this petitions.

I observe you [Congress] are loaded with petitions from the manufacturing, commercial and agricultural interests, each praying you to sacrifice the others to them. This proves the egoism of the whole and happily balances their cannibal appetites to eat one another.

* * * I do not know whether it is any part of the petitions of the farmers that our citizens shall be restrained to eat nothing but bread, because that can be made here. But this is the common spirit of all their petitions.[289]

Some jealousy of this spirit of manufacture seems excited among commercial men. It would have been as

---

[287] The Anas #1523 (1792.)
[288] The Anas #1525 (1818.)
[289] To Hugh Nelson #7081 (M., 1820.)

ON THE ECONOMY

just when we first began to make our own plows & hoes. They have certainly lost the profit of bringing these from a foreign country.

You are a free trade advocate, but chose an embargo hoping to not have a war with Europe, because of the European nations seeing our ships and sailors as free game, that every neutral vessel found on the high seas, whatsoever be her cargo, and whatsoever foreign port be that of her departure or destination, shall be deemed lawful prize. The German, French and English edicts created the blockade of our foreign commerce and navigation.

My idea is that we should encourage home manufactures to the extent of our own consumption of every thing of which we raise the raw material. I do not think it fair in the shipowners to say we ought not to make our own axes, nails, &c., here that they may have the benefit of carrying the iron to Europe, & bringing back the axes, nails, &c. Our agriculture will still afford surplus produce enough to employ a due proportion of navigation.[290]

Although a free trade advocate, I am glad to see you desire manufacturing at home. Sam Walton, the founder of Walmart, promoted "Buy American" and promoted little manufacturing business in small towns. His store became a world leader, but then moved to buy at the cheapest price. Foreign imports from China and Southeast Asia grew and the small manufacturers in America closed.

---

[290] To David Humphreys, LOC (W., Jan. 20, 1809.)
http://hdl.loc.gov/loc.mss/mtj.mtjbib019612

It is our business to manufacture for ourselves whatever we can, to keep our markets open for what we can spare or want.[291] In general, it is impossible that manufactures should succeed in America from the high price of labor.[292]

We have all sorts of government organizations promoting American business in the United States and around the world, but labor is cheaper in foreign lands and quality has declined purposefully, so items must be replaced. There is a fine line between shareholders making a profit, the CEO making his tens of millions, and the consumer getting a product that lasts long enough that it cannot be returned to the merchant.

The merchants will manage commerce the better, the more they are left free to manage for themselves.[293]

I am for free commerce with all nations.[294] All the world is becoming commercial. Were it practicable to keep our new empire separated from them, we might indulge ourselves in speculating whether commerce contributes to the happiness of mankind. But we cannot separate ourselves from them. Our citizens have had too full a taste of the comforts furnished by the arts and manufactures to be debarred the use of them. We must, then, in our defence endeavor to share as large a portion as we can of this modern source of wealth and power.[295]

---

[291] To Thomas Leiper #5017 (M., 1815.)
[292] To Thomas Digges #5036 (P., 1788.)
[293] To Gideon Granger #5161 (M., 1800.)
[294] To Elbridge Gerry #3254 (Pa., 1799.)
[295] To General Washington #1394 (A., 1784.)

Our interest will be to throw open the doors of commerce, and to knock off all its shackles, giving perfect freedom to all persons for the vent of whatever they may choose to bring into our ports, and asking the same in theirs.[296]

But you chose an embargo, hampering and providing hardships to many businesses and American Citizens.

The communications now made [to Congress] showing the great and increasing dangers with which our vessels, our seamen, and merchandise, are threatened on the high seas, and elsewhere, from the belligerent powers of Europe, and it being of great importance to keep in safety these essential resources, I deem it my duty to recommend the subject to the consideration of Congress, who will doubtless perceive all the advantages which may be expected from an inhibition of the departure of our vessels from the ports of the United States. Their wisdom will also see the necessity of making every preparation for whatever events may grow out of the present crisis.[297] *The alternative was between that [an embargo] and war, and, in fact, it is the last card we have to play, short of war.*[298]

I am glad to see that you went to Congress rather than taking it upon yourself with what is now called and "Executive Order". This embargo, I presume, was enacted on and in due time was lifted. Was anything gained besides averting war?

---

[296] Notes on Virginia #3249 (1782.)
[297] Special Message #2511 (Dec. 18, 1807.)
[298] To Levi Lincoln #2514 (W., March 1808.)

Amidst the pressure of evils with which the belligerent edicts have afflicted us, some permanent good will arise. The spring given to manufactures will have durable effects. Knowing most of my own state, I can affirm with confidence that were free intercourse opened again tomorrow she would never again import one half of the coarse goods which she has done down to the date of the edicts. These will be made in our families. For finer goods we must resort to the larger manufactories established in the towns.[299]

Regarding Executive Orders, I would assume the Louisiana purchase could be consider one. Besides the purchase not having a constitutional basis, it added a considerable amount of debt to the United States.

While I was in Europe, I purchased everything I could lay my hands on which related to any part of America, and particularly had a pretty full collection of the English, French, and Spanish authors on the subject of Louisiana.[300]

So you had knowledge of the value of Louisiana to the United States?

*The cession of Louisiana and the Floridas by Spain to France, works most sorely on the United States. * * * There is on the globe one single spot, the possessor of which is our natural and habitual enemy. It is New Orleans, through which the produce of three-eighths*

---

[299] To David Humphreys, LOC (W., Jan. 20, 1809.)
    http://hdl.loc.gov/loc.mss/mtj.mtjbib019612
[300] To William Dunbar #3738 (W., 1804.)

of our territory must pass to market, and from its fertility it will ere long yield more than half of our whole produce, and contain more than half of our inhabitants. France, placing herself in that door, assumes to us the attitude of defiance.[301]

The cutting off of the port of New Orleans and the concern of France's nation building west of the Mississippi was the concern for your action.

Congress witnessed, at their last session, the extraordinary agitation produced in the public mind by the suspension of our right of deposit at the port of New Orleans, no assignment of another place having been made according to treaty. They were sensible that the continuance of that privation would be more injurious to our nation than any consequences which could flow from any mode of redress, but reposing just confidence in the good faith of the government whose officer had committed the wrong, friendly and reasonable representations were resorted to, and the right of deposit was restored.

Previous, however, to this period, we had not been unaware of the danger to which our peace would be perpetually exposed while so important a key to the commerce of the western country remained under foreign power. Difficulties, too, were presenting themselves as to the navigation of other streams, which, arising within territories, pass through those adjacent. Propositions had, therefore, been authorized

---

[301] To Robert R. Livingston #4826 (April 1802.)

for obtaining, on fair conditions, the sovereignty of New Orleans, and of other possessions in that quarter interesting to our quiet, to such extent as was deemed practicable; and the provisional appropriation of two millions of dollars, to be applied and accounted for by the President of the United States, intended as part of the price, was considered as conveying the sanction of Congress to the acquisition proposed.[302]

So Congress approved two million dollars for the purchase of New Orleans, and you spent fifteen million dollars, when New Orleans and all of Louisiana, clear to the Rockies, was offered by Napoleon's representatives.

The Constitution has made no provision for our holding foreign territory, still less for incorporating foreign nations into our Union. The Executive in seizing the fugitive occurrence [Louisiana purchase] which so much advances the good of their country, have done an act beyond the Constitution. The Legislature in casting behind them metaphysical subtleties, and risking themselves like faithful servants, must ratify and pay for it, and throw themselves on their country for doing for them unauthorized, what we know they would have done for themselves had they been in a situation to do it.

It is the case of a guardian, investing the money of his ward in purchasing an important adjacent territory; and saying to him when of age, I did this for your good; I pretend to no right to bind you: you may

[302] Third Annual Message #4798 (October 17, 1803.)

disavow me, and I must get out of the scrape as I can: I thought it my duty to risk myself for you. But we shall not be disavowed by the nation, and their act of indemnity will confirm and not weaken the Constitution, by more strongly marking out its lines.[303]

Most thought it was a great acquisition, but you did have Federalist opponents who thought it was outrageous, that it would support the common people opposed to big government and their ideology. The Party rather than the people.

*The less that is said about any constitutional difficulty, the better; and * * * it will be desirable for Congress to do what is necessary, in silence.*[304] *Whatever Congress shall think it necessary to do, should be done with as little debate as possible, and particularly so far as respects the constitutional difficulty. I am aware of the force of the observations you make on the power given by the Constitution to Congress, to admit new States into the Union, without restraining the subject to the territory then constituting the United States. But when I consider that the limits of the United States are precisely fixed by the treaty of 1783, that the Constitution expressly declares itself to be made for the United States, I cannot help believing that the intention was to permit Congress to admit into the Union new States, which should be formed out of the territory for which, and under whose authority alone, they were then acting.*

---

[303] To John C. Breckenridge #4807 (M., Aug. 12, 1803.)
[304] To Levi Lincoln #4811 (M., Aug. 1803.)

I do not believe it was meant that they might receive England, Ireland, Holland, &c., into it, which would be the case on your construction. When an instrument admits two constructions, the one safe, the other dangerous; the one precise, the ether indefinite, I prefer that which is safe and precise. I had rather ask an enlargement of power from the nation, where it is found necessary, than to assume it by a construction which would make our powers boundless. Our peculiar security is in the possession of a written Constitution. Let us not make it a blank paper by construction. I say the same as to the opinion of those who consider the grant of the treaty making power as boundless. If it is, then we have no Constitution. If it has bounds, they can be no others than the definitions of the powers which that instrument gives. It specifies and delineates the operations permitted to the Federal Government, and gives all the powers necessary to carry these into execution.

Whatever of these enumerated objects is proper for a law, Congress may make the law; whatever is proper to be executed by way of a treaty, the President and Senate may enter into the treaty; whatever is to be done by a judicial sentence, the judges may pass the sentence. Nothing is more likely than that their enumeration of powers is defective. This is the ordinary case of all human works. Let us go on, then, perfecting it, by adding, by way of amendment to the Constitution, those powers which time and trial show are still wanting. But it has been taken too much for granted, that by this rigorous construction the treaty power would be reduced to nothing.

I had occasion once to examine its effect on the French treaty, made by the old Congress, and found that out of thirty odd articles which that contained, there were one, two or three only which could not now be stipulated under our present Constitution. I confess, then, I thought it important, in the present case, to set an example against broad construction, by appealing for new power to the people. If, however, our friends shall think differently, certainly I shall acquiesce with satisfaction; confiding, that the good sense of our country will correct the evil of construction whenever it shall produce ill effects.[305]

Mr. Jefferson, I know a whole book could be done on the Louisiana purchase, but it seems you admit that you overstepped your constitutional bounds with the knowledge and consent of at least some of Congress. Fortunately Congress backed you on adding thirteen million dollars of debt and doubling the land size of the United States. We have continued to add territories since you set the example.

When we contemplate the ordinary annual augmentation of imposts from increasing population and wealth, the augmentation of the same revenue by its extension to the new acquisition, and the economies which may still be introduced into our public expenditures, I cannot but hope that Congress in reviewing their resources will find means to meet the interme-

---

[305] To Wilson C. Nicholas #4812 (M., Sep. 1803.)

diate interests of this additional debt without recurring to new taxes, and applying to this object only the ordinary progression of our revenue.[306]

So you did not believe taxes would need to be raised, that those in the new Louisiana Territory would pay the debt. And to think, that with your rule, that all debts at that time had to be paid within the generation causing the debt, about eighteen years, that Louisiana would be paid for.

On great occasions every good officer must be ready to risk himself in going beyond the strict line of law, when the public preservation requires it; his motives will be a justification as far as there is any discretion in his ultra-legal proceedings, and no indulgence of private feelings.[307]

The Territory of Louisiana was to pay for itself. But now, we have, Illinois, home state of President Obama, and Puerto Rico, a territory since 1898, that are desiring to be bailed out because of their gross overspending and mismanagement.

*The assumption of State debts has appeared as revolting to several States as their non-assumption to others. It is proposed to strip the proposition of the injustice it would have done by leaving the States who have redeemed much of their debts on no better footing than those who have redeemed none * * * I have been, and still am of their opinion that Congress should always prefer letting the States raise money in*

---

[306] Third Annual Message #4849 (Oct. 1803.)
[307] To Governor Claiborne #4529 (W., 1807.)

their own way, where it can be done. But, in the present instance, I see the necessity of yielding for this time to the cries of the creditors in certain parts of the Union; for the sake of Union, and to save us from the greatest of all calamities, the total extinction of our credit in Europe.[308]

That may be true for the paying off of the Revolutionary War debt, as it was for the benefit of all, but I do not think you would agree to it, if you knew it was to provide extravagance which the other states would not spend on, such as high salaries, early retirements, and this they bragged about.

Now it seems the norm for Executive Orders to cost millions without Congressional approval. President Obama's 1% pay increase in December 2014, authorized under a law concerning "national emergency or serious economic conditions" takes $2.5 billion dollars from other spending across the federal budget, and the real thing that makes this bad Mr. Jefferson, is that we are not under a national emergency and the President tells on the news that we have a great economy.

The subject of the debates was, whether the representatives of the people were to have no check on the expenditure of the public money, and the Executive to squander it at their will, leaving to the Legislature only the drudgery of furnishing the money. They begin to open their eyes on this to the Eastward, and to suspect they have been hoodwinked.[309]

---

[308] To James Monroe #580 (N. Y., June 1790.)
[309] To Edmund Pendleton #1532 (Pa., April 1798.)

Unless the mass retains sufficient control over those entrusted with the powers of their government, these will be perverted to their own oppression, and to the perpetuation of wealth and power in the individuals and their families selected for the trust.[310] If we can prevent the government from wasting the labors of the people, under the pretence of taking care of them, they must become happy.[311]

What do you think about the government getting into the day to day workings of public works?

*Private enterprise manages * * * much better [than the government] all the concerns to which it is equal.[312]*

Why do you think that private enterprise manages better.

*I received your favor covering an offer; of an iron mine to the public, and I thank you for * * * making the communication * * *. But having always observed that public works are much less advantageously managed than they are by private hands, I have thought it better for the public to go to market for whatever it wants which is to be found there; for there competition brings it down to the minimum of value. I have no doubt we can buy brass cannon at market cheaper than we could make iron ones. I think it material, too, not to abstract the high executive officers from those functions which nobody else is*

---

310 To Mr. Van der Kemp #6837 (M., 1812.)
311 To Thomas Cooper #2847 (W., 1802.)
312 Sixth Annual Message #6458 (1806.)

*charged to carry on, and to employ them in superin-
tending works which are going on abundantly in private hands. Our predecessors went on different principles; they bought iron mines, and sought for copper
ones. We own a mine at Harper's Ferry of the finest
iron ever put into a cannon, which we are afraid to
attempt to work. We have rented it heretofore, but it
is now without a tenant.*[313]

Do you believe that the United States should be in the business of promoting some industries over others? President
Obama had an Executive Order to cut carbon dioxide emis-
sions which put many coal fired generating plants out of
business, which then hurt the coal mines and miners. From
there, the damage continues to the local schools and governments, to the stores. He also has Executive Orders to promote wind and solar energy.

*The policy of the American government is to leave
their citizens free, neither restraining nor aiding
them in their pursuits.*[314]

*The New Orleans Canal Company ask specifically
that we should loan them $50,000, or take the remain-
ing fourth of their shares now on hand. This last
measure is too much out of our policy of not embark-
ing the public in enterprises better managed by individuals, and which might occupy as much of our time
as those political duties for which the public functionaries are particularly instituted. Some money*

---

[313] To Mr. Bibb #5242 (M., July 1808.)
[314] To M. L'Hommande #4684 (P., 1787.)

could be lent them, but only on an assurance that it would be employed so as to secure the public objects.[315]

I wish you would have been around during our Panic of 2008, which became the Great Recession. It started as a bank run on AIG overseas. President George Bush and then President Obama bailed out the big banks and insurance companies due to sales of credit default swaps and subprime mortgages. With the bailout of the financial institutions the government thought "to big to fail", the government took stock in the companies. General Motors and Chrysler also failed. Congress turned down a bailout loan for them. Going through a twisted bankruptcy, the creditors were not awarded deficiency claims. When the companies were given the funds by the Executive Branch to start back up, out of the "Tarp Funds," a fund for financial institution's bailout, it had not been approved by Congress. The Federal Government and the United Auto Workers Union ended up owning much of the company's stock. It ended up costing the American citizen's Treasury billions of dollars.

The functions of the Executive are not competent to the decision of questions of property between individuals. They are ascribed to the Judiciary alone, and when either persons or property are taken into their custody, there is no power in this country that can take them out.[316]

---

[315] To Governor Claiborne #7107 (W., July 1808.)
[316] To Edmond Charles Genet #7040 (Pa., 1793.)

So you are saying that instead of the President's administration doing the refinance, it should have been handled by the courts under bankruptcy laws.

At length our paper bubble is burst. The failure of Duer [a large banker], in New York, soon brought on others, and these still more, like nine pins knocking one another down, till at that place the bankruptcy is become general. Every man concerned in paper being broke, and most of the tradesmen and farmers, who had been laying down money, having been tempted by these speculators to lend it to them at an interest of from 3 to 6 percent, a month, have lost the whole.[317] The losses on this occasion would support a war such as we now have on hand, five or six years.[318]

The evidences of the public debt are solid and sacred. I presume there is not a man in the United States who would not part with his last shilling to pay them. But all that stuff called scrip, of whatever description, was folly or roguery, and under a resemblance to genuine public paper, it buoyed itself up to a par with that. It has given a severe lesson; yet such is the public gullibility in the hands of cunning and unprincipled men, that it is doomed by nature to receive these lessons once in an age at least. Happy if they now come about and get back into the tract of plain unsophisticated common sense which they ought never to have been decoyed from.[319]

[317] To T. M. Randolph #6336 (Pa., 1792.)
[318] To William Short #6335 (Pa., April 1792.)
[319] To Francis Eppes #6333 (Pa., April 1792.)

I like your idea of coming back to common sense. Do we need it now! The stuff you call scrip was the cause of the Panic of 2008. There was financial executives, testifying before Congress, that the paper they were selling was worthless, that the buyers should have known better. We now have people buying what is called Bitcoin, a virtual digital currency which is being used by some as decentralized money. Again not backed by anything but somebodies smile. The Federal Government again falls away from the constitution on the matter of money. Do they not learn from previous failures?

Capital may be produced by industry, and accumulated by economy; but jugglers only will propose to create it by legerdemain tricks with paper.[320] *I told the President [Washington] that a system had there [in the Treasury Department] been contrived for deluging the States with paper money instead of gold and silver, for withdrawing our citizens from the pursuits of commerce, manufactures, buildings, and other branches of useful industry, to occupy themselves and their capitals in a species of gambling, destructive of morality, and which had introduced its poison into the government itself.*[321]

I always thought the best way to create capital was from mining gold and silver. The Federal Government and some states have put a damper on that too, in various states and on Federal land. Small time mining helped many individuals through the depression and other times in our history, including now.

---

320 To J. W. Eppes #1127 (M., Nov. 1813.)
321 The Anas #3946 (Feb. 1792.)

The citizens of a country like ours will never have unemployed capital. Too many enterprises are open, offering high profits, to permit them to lend their capitals on a regular and moderate interest. They are too enterprising and sanguine themselves not to believe they can do better with it.[322]

Money is the agent by which modern nations will recover their rights.[323] *By the Constitution Congress may regulate the value of foreign coin; but if they do not do it, the old power revives to the State, the Constitution only forbidding them to make anything but gold and silver a tender in payment of debts.*[324] *I deny the power of the General Government of making paper money, or anything else, a legal tender.*[325] *Paper [money] is liable to be abused, has been, is, and forever will be abused, in every country in which it is permitted.*[326]

Mr. Jefferson, China has been acquiring gold to establish their currency as the stable money of the world. I think China will need a change of ideology with the gold to become the world reserve currency. You were never much on paper money or financial paper, but you do like plain paper.

This article, the creature of art, and but latterly so comparatively, is now interwoven so much into the

---

[322] To President Madison #1128 (M., 1815.)
[323] To Comte de Moustier #5385 (P., 1788.)
[324] To John Taylor #5381 (Pa., 1797.)
[325] To John Taylor #5383 (M., 1798.)
[326] To J. W. Eppes #6340 (M., Nov. 1813.)

conveniences and occupations of men, as to have be-come one of the necessaries of civilized life.[327]

Do you think the government owes a person his livelihood and welfare?

I conscientiously believe that governments founded in republican principles are more friendly to the happi-ness of the people at large, and especially of a people so capable of self-government as ours.[328]

To constrain the brute force of the people, the Euro-pean governments deem it necessary to keep them down by hard labor, poverty and ignorance, and to take from them, as from bees, so much of their earn-ings, as that unremitting labor shall be necessary to obtain a sufficient surplus to sustain a scanty and miserable life.[329]

That sounds like the Democrats now. They are the tax and spend Party, keeping the citizens dependent on the govern-ment for everything. The government was missing support-ing the college goers for a while, but they have now caught them with the college loans available to everyone. As more money went out in loans, the colleges kept raising their rates. The students had to borrow more, and the rates continued to go up. Students get out of college now and spend their life trying to pay the loans off. Now, the Democrats want to for-give the trillion dollars of debt. Of course it is not their money paying it off so it is no big deal.

---

[327] To Robert R. Livingston #6339 (Pa., 1800.)
[328] To David Howell #7329 (M., 1810.)
[329] To William Johnson #4306 (M., 1823.)

I think we have more machinery of government than is necessary, too many parasites living on the labor of the industrious. I believe it might be much simplified to the relief of those who maintain it. [330] The true foundation of republican government is the equal right of every citizen, in his person and property, and in their management.[331]

What you like is life, liberty and the pursuit of happiness, as you put it into a latter draft of the Declaration of Independence.

The most fortunate of us, in our journey through life, frequently meet with calamities and misfortunes which may greatly afflict us; and, to fortify our minds against the attacks of these calamities and misfortunes, should be one of the principal studies and endeavors of our lives. The only method of doing this is to assume a perfect resignation to the Divine will, to consider that whatever does happen, must happen; and that, by our uneasiness, we cannot prevent the blow before it does fall, but we may add to its force after it has fallen.

These considerations, and others such as these, may enable us in some measure to surmount the difficulties thrown in our way; to bear up with a tolerable degree of patience under this burden of life; and to proceed with a pious and unshaken resignation, till we arrive at our journeys end, when we may deliver up our trust into the hands of Him who gave it, and

---

330 To William Ludlow #3571 (M., 1824.)
331 To Samuel Kerchival #3507 (M., 1816.)

receive such reward as to Him shall seem propor-tioned to our merit. Such will be the language of the man who considers his situation in this life, and such should be the language of every man who would wish to render that situation as easy as the nature of it will admit. Few things will disturb him at all: nothing will disturb him much.[332]

This is true Mr. Jefferson, but do you think we should take care of those needing help or those who are unable to work?

Private charities, as well as contributions to public purposes in proportion to every one's circumstances, are certainly among the duties we owe to society.[333]

But is it the governments duty?

We are all doubtless bound to contribute a certain portion of our income to the support of charitable and other useful public institutions. But it is a part of our duty also to apply our contributions in the most effec-tual way we can to secure their object.

The question, then, is whether this will not be better done by each of us appropriating our whole contribu-tions to the institutions within our reach, under our own eye; and over which we can exercise some useful control? Or, would it be better that each should divide the sum he can spare among all the institutions of his State, or of the United States? Reason, and the interest

---

[332] To John Page #7405 (S., 1763.)
[333] To Charles Christian #1195 (M., 1812.)

of these institutions themselves, certainly decide in favor of the former practice.

This question has been forced on me, heretofore, by the multitude of applications which have come to me from every quarter of the Union on behalf of academies, churches, missions, hospitals, charitable establishments, &c. Had I parcelled among them all the contributions which I could spare, it would have been for each too feeble a sum to be worthy of being either given or received. If each portion of the State, on the contrary, will apply its aids and its attentions exclusively to those nearest around them, all will be better taken care of. Their support, their conduct, and the best administration of their funds, will be under the inspection and control of those most convenient to take cognizance of them, and most interested in their prosperity.[334]

So Mr. Jefferson, you think welfare should be local, to see that it in being properly used. You do think people should work if they can?

If we can prevent the government from wasting the labors of the people, under the pretence of taking care of them, they must become happy.[335] To preserve the peace of our fellow citizens, promote their prosperity and happiness, reunite opinion, cultivate a spirit of candor, moderation, charity and forbearance toward one another, are objects calling for the efforts and

---

[334] To Samuel Kerchival #1196 (M., 1810.)
[335] To Thomas Cooper #2358 (W., 1802.)

---

sacrifices of every good man and patriot. Our religion enjoins it; our happiness demands it; and no sacrifice is requisite but of passions hostile to both.[336]

Everyone has a natural right to choose that vocation in life which he thinks most likely to give him comfortable subsistence.[337]

Nothing can contribute more to your future happiness (moral rectitude always excepted), than the contracting a habit of industry and activity. Of all the cankers of human happiness none corrodes with so silent, yet so baneful an influence as indolence. Body and mind both unemployed, our being becomes a burden, and every object about us loathsome, even the dearest. Idleness begets ennui [melancholy], ennui the hypochondriac, and that a diseased body.[338] *In a world which furnishes so many employments which are so useful, so many which are amusing, it is our own fault if we ever know what ennui is, or if we are driven to the miserable resources of gaming, which corrupts our dispositions, and teaches us a habit of hostility against all mankind.*[339]

So it sounds like you are against gaming. It is the fairly new fad in the United States to have gaming and lotteries to help support States. Many States use it to help support programs such as education.

---

[336] To the Rhode Island Assembly #9063 (W., 1801.)
[337] Thoughts on Lotteries #5690 (M., Feb. 1826.)
[338] To Martha Jefferson #3821 (1787.)
[339] To Martha Jefferson #3822 (1787.)

Having myself made it a rule never to engage in a lottery or any other adventure of mere chance, I can, with the less candor or effect, urge it on others, however laudable or desirable its object may be.[340]

During the past decade or two, there has been a strong government push to take control of citizen's property. The reasons may be to stop a use of the property due to a mouse or a snail darter that environmentalists want to protect, the Clean Water Act, or even the government allowing for eminent domain for another citizen to develop the property held by the first, to get more tax money. Governments employ all sorts of manners in taking control of the property. Grant you, some are needed for roads and infrastructure, but what about the rest?

By nature's law, every man has a right to seize and retake by force, his own property, taken from him by another, by force or fraud. Nor is this natural right among the first which is taken into the hands of regular government, after it is instituted. It was long retained by our ancestors. It was a part of their common law, laid down in their Books, recognized by all the authorities, and regulated as to circumstances of practice.[341]

It is a dangerous lesson to say to the people "whenever your functionaries exercise unlawful authority over you, if you do not go into actual resistance, it will be deemed acquiescence and confirmation." How

---

[340] To Hugh L. White #4797 (M., 1810.)
[341] Batture Case #7050 (1812.)

long had we acquiesced under usurpations of the Brit-ish parliament? Had that confirmed them in right, and made our Revolution a wrong? Besides no authority has yet decided whether this resistance must be instantaneous: when the right to resist ceases, or whether it has yet ceased?[342]

Mr. Jefferson, you are saying just because Federal abuses have been happening, it does not mean the citizens approve of the injustices, but are waiting for a better time to correct them.

I consider the people who constitute a society or nation as the source of all authority in that nation; as free to transact their common concerns by any agents they think proper; to change these agents in-dividually, or the organization of them in form or function whenever they please; that all the acts done by these agents under the authority of the nation are the acts of the nation, are obligatory to them and inure to their use, and can in no wise be annulled or affected by any change in the form of the govern-ment, or of the persons administering it.[343]

You have overstepped your executive authority as President in the purchase of the Louisiana Territory and some would say the Embargo may have financially hurt many American businesses and citizens and then Batture Case in Louisiana, against one individual.

---

[342] To John Hambden Pleasants #640 (M., 1824.)
[343] Opinion on French Treaties #643 (1793.)

I have no pretensions to exemption from error. In a long course of public duties, I must have committed many. And I have reason to be thankful that, passing over these, an act of duty has been selected as a subject of complaint, which the delusions of self interest alone could have classed among them, and in which, were there error, it has been hallowed by the benedictions of an entire province, an interesting member of our national family, threatened with destruction by the bold enterprise of one individual.[344]

Fortitude teaches us to meet and surmount difficulties; not to fly from them, like cowards; and to fly, too, in vain, for they will meet and arrest us at every turn of our road. Fortitude is one of the four cardinal virtues of Epicurus.[345]

What do you think about a balanced budget?

I place economy among the first and most important of republican virtues, and public debt as the greatest of the dangers to be feared.[346]

*I wish it were possible to obtain a single amendment to our Constitution. I would be willing to depend on that alone for the reduction of the administration of our government to the genuine principles of its Constitution; I mean an additional article, taking from the Federal Government the power of borrowing. * * * I know that to pay all proper expenses within the*

---

[344] The Batture Case #2730 (1812.)

[345] To William Short #3101 (M., 1819.)

[346] To Governor Plumer #2049 (M., 1816.)

year, would, in case of war, be hard on us. But not so hard as ten wars instead of one. For wars could be reduced in that proportion; besides that the State governments would be free to lend their credit in borrowing quotas. [347]

One of the big issues now is Global Warming. Records show global warming was not happening so now they call it Climate Change. A few of the leaders from President Clinton's era came up with this to make money. They continue threatening our economy and way of life. What I find crazy, is that in the 1970's, we were warned of the impending Ice Age.

The change which has taken place in our climate, is one of those facts which all men of years are sensible of, and yet none can prove by regular evidence; they can only appeal to each other's general observation for the fact. I remember when I was a small boy (say sixty years ago), snows were frequent and deep in every winter to my knee very often, to my waist sometimes and that they covered the earth long. And I remember while yet young, to have heard from very old men, that in their youth, the winters had been still colder, with deeper and longer snows. In the year 1772, we had a snow two feet deep in the champaign parts of Virginia, and three feet in the counties next below the mountains. That year is still marked in conversation by the designation of "the year of the deep snow." But I know of no regular diaries of the weather very far back. In latter times, they might perhaps be found. While I lived at Washington, I kept

---

[347] To John Taylor #4787 (M., Nov. 1798.)

a diary, and by recurring to that, I observe that from the winter of 1802-3, to that of 1808-9, inclusive, the average fall of snow of the seven winters was only fourteen and a half inches, and that the ground was covered but sixteen days in each winter on an average of the whole. The maximum in any one winter, during that period, was twenty-one inches fall, and thirty-four days on the ground.[348]

So from time to time you had change too. I guess they cannot blame our cars and asthma inhalers for it. It sounds to me more like, "let's find a reason to invest in drug companies, and require the generic asthma inhalers to be reformulated and be no longer generic. Let's make money off of climate change." And from there it went to wind and solar. Sorry, Mr. Jefferson, it just aggravates me so much that a government of the people, really isn't.

Before we move on to taxation, is there anything else you would like to say about the economy and what we need in the upcoming election?

I think all the world would gain by setting commerce at perfect liberty.[349] *Restrain men from injuring one another, * * * [but] leave them otherwise free to regulate their own pursuits of industry and improvement.*[350] *We shall push Congress to the uttermost in economizing. A rigid economy of the public contributions, and absolute interdiction of all useless expenses, will go far towards keeping the government honest*

---

[348] To Dr. Chapman #1325 (M., 1809.)
[349] To John Adams #3250 (July 1785.)
[350] First Inaugural Address #3948 (1801.)

and unoppressive.[351] *We must make our election between economy and liberty, or profusion and servitude.*[352]

[351] To Marquis Lafayette #2359 (M., 1823.)
[352] To Samuel Kerchival #2362 (M., 1816.)

ON DEBT

The accounts of the United States ought to be, and may be made, as simple as those of a common farmer, and capable of being understood by common farmers.[353]

I am for a government rigorously frugal and simple, applying all the possible savings of the public revenue to the discharge of the national debt.[354]

The principle of spending money to be paid by posterity, under the name of funding, is but swindling futurity on a large scale.[355]

Unfortunately, the finances of the United States are very complicated and we are swindling our future generations with a huge debt.

---

[353] To James Madison #39 (M., 1796.)
[354] To Elbridge Gerry #2369 (Pa., 1799.)
[355] To John Taylor #3328 (M., 1816.)

That our Creator made the earth for the use of the living and not of the dead; that those who exist not can have no use nor right in it, no authority or power over it; that one generation of men cannot foreclose or burthen its use to another, which comes to it in its own right and by the same divine beneficence; that a preceding generation cannot bind a succeeding one by its laws or contracts; these deriving their obligation from the will of the existing majority, and that majority being removed by death, another comes in its place with a will equally free to make its own laws and contracts; these are axioms so self-evident that no explanation can make them plainer; for he is not to be reasoned with who says that non-existence can control existence, or that nothing can move something.

They are axioms also pregnant with salutary consequences. The laws of civil society, indeed, for the encouragement of industry, give the property of the parent to his family on his death, and in most civilized countries permit him even to give it, by testament, to whom he pleases. And it is also found more convenient to suffer the laws of our predecessors to stand on our implied assent, as if positively reenacted, until the existing majority positively repeals them. But this does not lessen the right of that majority to repeal whenever a change of circumstances or of will calls for it. Habit alone confounds what is civil practice with natural right.[356]

---

[356] To Thomas Earle #3401 (M., 1823.)

There are taxes at death and even taxes when giving money away, if it is a large enough amount. We will be indebted by Twenty trillion dollars in actual paper in the Spring of 2017, the amount nearly doubling in Obama's eight years as President. The United States also has promised another 30 to 128 trillion dollars in unfunded liabilities for things such as Social Security and Medicare. Then with the Federal Reserve Banks, and their control of the money supply and interest rates, it starts to get things really jumbled.

A rigid economy of the public contributions, and absolute interdiction of all useless expenses, will go far towards keeping the government honest and unoppressive.[357]

The Debt when you first took office as President was approximately eighty three million dollars, about 2.82 billion dollars in 2015 dollars, and was about sixty five million dollars when you left office. That was also the period where you paid fifteen million for the Louisiana Territory. You brought the debt down. Great work, Mr. Jefferson.

*If * * * [there] can be added a simplification of the form of accounts in the Treasury department, and in the organization of its officers, so as to bring everything to a single centre, we might hope to see the finances of the Union as clear and intelligible as a merchant's books, so that every member of Congress, and every man of any mind in the Union, should be able to comprehend them, to investigate abuses, and consequently to control them.*

---

[357] To Marquis Lafayette #2359 (M., 1823.)

Our predecessors have endeavored by intricacies of system, and shuffling the investigation over from one officer to another, to cover everything from detection. I hope we shall go in the contrary direction, and that, by our honest and judicious reformations, we may be able in the limits of our time, to bring things back to that simple and intelligible system, on which they should have been organized at first.[358]

The finances of our nation are abominable. You helped to simplify the Treasury as President, maybe there is hope that our new President take back the Treasury to the earlier principles.

The Constitution says, "Congress shall have power to lay and collect taxes, duties, imposts, and excises, to pay the debts, &c., provide for the common defence and general welfare of the United States". I suppose the meaning of this clause to be, that Congress may collect taxes for the purpose of providing for the general welfare, in those cases wherein the Constitution empowers them to act for the general welfare. To suppose that it was meant to give them a distinct substantive power, to do any act which might tend to the general welfare, is to render all the enumerations useless, and to make their powers unlimited.[359]

Mr. Jefferson, the "General Welfare" clause continues to come up as a major issue to the United States' problems. It is the cause of our major debts nowadays, by continuing to add

---

[358] To Albert Gallatin #40 (W., 1802.)
[359] Opinion on Fugitive Slaves #3392 (Dec. 1792.)

on programs, because they have the endless supply of money for debt. Congress just votes to increase the debt limit. Then the confusion and mistrust of the government and the Treasury does not help things.

*Alexander Hamilton * * * in order that he might have the entire government of his [Treasury] machine, determined so to complicate it as that neither the President nor Congress should be able to understand it, or to control him. He succeeded in doing this, not only beyond their reach, but so that he at length could not unravel it himself. He gave to the debt, in the first instance, in funding it, the most artificial and mysterious form he could devise. He then moulded up his appropriations of a number of scraps and remnants, many of which were nothing at all, and applied them to different objects in reversion and remainder, until the whole system was involved in impenetrable fog; and while he was giving himself the airs of providing for the payment of the debt, he left himself free to add to it continually, as he did in fact, instead of paying it.[360]*

The Treasury machine continues to fog our economy.

At the time we were funding our national debt, we heard much about "a public debt being a public blessing"; that the stock representing it was a creation of active capital for the aliment of commerce, manufactures and agriculture. This paradox was well adapted to the minds of believers in dreams, and the gulls of

---

[360] To Albert Gallatin #36 (W., 1801.)

that size entered bond fide into it. But the art and mystery of banks is a wonderful improvement on that. It is established on the principle that "private debts are a public blessing"; that the evidences of those private debts, called bank notes, become active capital, and aliment the whole commerce, manufactures, and agriculture of the United States.

Active capital is the sustenance of all industries, but is it proper to create the money from creating an endless debt?

Here are a set of people, for instance, who have bestowed on us the great blessing of running in our debt about two hundred millions of dollars, without our knowing who they are, where they are, or want property they have to pay this debt when called on; nay, who have made us so sensible of the blessings of letting them run in our debt, that we have exempted them by law from the repayment of these debts beyond a given proportion (generally estimated at one-third).

And to fill up the measure of blessing, instead of paying, they receive an interest on what they owe from those to whom they owe; for all the notes, or evidences of what they owe, which we see in circulation, have been lent to somebody on an interest which is levied again on us through the medium of commerce. And they are so ready still to deal out their liberalities to us, that they are now willing to let themselves run in our debt ninety millions more, on our paying them the same premium of six or eight per cent, interest, and on the same legal exemption from the repayment of more than thirty millions of the debt when it shall be called for. [361]

It is like the "robbing of Peter to pay Paul" expression.

The simple question appears to me to be what did the public owe, principal and interest, when the Secretary's taxes began to run? If less, it must have been paid; but if he was paying old debts with one hand and creating new ones with the other, it is such a game. [362]

That is how we are now over nineteen trillion dollars of debt now, and borrowing about fifty thousand dollars per second. It is time Congress gets control of their spending. They cannot blame it on the President as I read the Constitution.

But let us look at this principle in its original form, and its copy will then be equally understood. "A public debt is a public blessing." That our debt was juggled from forty-three to eighty millions, and funded at that amount, according to this opinion a great public blessing, because the evidences of it could be vested in commerce, and thus converted into active capital, and then the more the debt was made to be, the more active capital was created. That is to say, the creditors could now employ in commerce the money due them from the public, and make from it an annual profit of five per cent, or four millions of

---

[361] To J. W. Eppes #686 (M., Nov. 1813.)
[362] To James Madison #2062 (M., Sep. 1792.)

dollars. But observe, that the public were at the same time paying on it an interest of exactly the same amount of four millions of dollars. Where, then, is the gain to either party, which makes it a public blessing? There is no change in the state of things, but of persons only.

A has a debt due to him from the public, of which he holds their certificate as evidence, and on which he is receiving an annual interest. He wishes, however, to have the money itself, and to go into business with it. B has an equal sum of money in business, but wishes now to retire, and live on the interest. He therefore gives it to A in exchange for A's certificates of public stock. Now, then, A has the money to employ in business, which B so employed before. B has the money on interest to live on, which A lived on before; and the public pays the interest to B which they paid to A before. Here is no new creation of capital, no additional money employed, nor even a change in the employment of a single dollar. The, only change is of place between A and B in which we discover no creation of capital, nor public blessing. Suppose, again, the public to owe nothing. Then A not having lent his money to the public, would be in possession of it himself, and would go into business without the previous operation of selling stock.

Here, again, the same quantity of capital is employed as in the former case, though no public debt exists. In neither case is there any creation of active capital, nor other difference than that there is a public debt in the first case, and none in the last; and we may safely ask which of the two situations is most truly a public blessing? If, then, a public debt be no public blessing, we may pronounce, à fortiori [with stronger reason], that a private one cannot be so.

If the debt which the banking companies owe be a blessing to anybody, it is to themselves alone, who are realizing a solid interest of eight or ten per cent, on it. As to the public, these companies have banished all our gold and silver medium, which, before their institution, we had without interest, which never could have perished in our hands, and would have been our salvation now in the hour of war; instead of which they have given us two hundred million of froth and bubble, on which we are to pay them heavy interest, until it shall vanish into air as the Morris notes did.

We are warranted, then, in affirming that this parody on the principle of "a public debt being a public blessing," and its mutation into the blessing of private instead of public debts, is as ridiculous as the original principle itself. In both cases, the truth is, that capital may be produced by industry, and accumulated by economy; but jugglers only will propose to create it by legerdemain tricks with paper.[363]

Mr. Jefferson, the trickery you discuss reminds me of the bankers and brokers testifying to Congress following the 2008 Great Recession.

---

[363] To Samuel Kerchival #2013 (M., 1816.)

Banking establishments are more dangerous than standing armies.[364]

It morphed with the real estate and mortgage crash. What is interesting to the trickery, was the bankers and brokers saying that they knew the paper (subprime mortgages) they were selling was worthless, but as long as there were suckers out there to buy it, the worthless paper made them richer.

What is to hinder [the government] from creating a perpetual debt? The laws of nature, I answer. The earth belongs to the living not to the dead. The will and the power of man expire with his life, by nature's law. Some societies give it an artificial continuance, for the encouragement of industry; some refuse it, as our aboriginal neighbors, whom we call barbarians. The generations of men may be considered as bodies or corporations. Each generation has the usufruct of the earth during the period of its continuance. When it ceases to exist the usufruct passes on to the succeeding generation, free and unincumbered, and so on, successively, from one generation to another forever.

We may consider each generation as a distinct nation, with a right, by the will of its majority, to bind themselves, but none to bind the succeeding generation, more than the inhabitants of another country. Or the case may be likened to the ordinary one of a tenant for life, who may hypothecate the land for his debts, during the continuance of his usufruct; but at his

---

[364] To John Taylor #689 (M., 1816.)

death, the reversioner (who is also for life only) receives it exonerated from all burden.

Unfortunately, Alexander Hamilton won out on the perpetual debt.

*The period of a generation, or the term of its life, is determined by the laws of mortality, which, varying a little only in different climates, offer a general average to be found by observation. * * * one-half will be dead in eighteen years and eight months. At nineteen years, then, from the date of a contract, the majority of the contractors are dead, and their contract with them. Let this general theory be applied to a particular case.*

Suppose that majority, on the first day of the year 1794, had borrowed a sum of money equal to the fee-simple value of the State, and to have consumed it in eating, drinking and making merry in their day; or, if you please, in quarrelling and fighting with their unoffending neighbors. Within eighteen years and eight months, one-half of the adult citizens were dead. Till then, being the majority, they might rightfully levy the interest of their debt annually on themselves and their fellow-revellers, or fellow-champions.

But at that period, say at this moment, a new majority have come into place, in their own right, and not under the rights, the conditions, or laws of their predecessors. Are they bound to acknowledge the debt, to consider the preceding generation as having had a right to eat up the whole soil of their country, in the course of a life, to alienate it from them (for it would be an alienation to the creditors), and would they think themselves either legally or morally bound to give up their country and emigrate to another for subsistence?

Every one will say no; that the soil is the gift of God to the living, as much as it had been to the deceased generation; and that the laws of nature impose no obligation on them to pay this debt. And although, like some other natural rights, this has not yet entered into any declaration of rights, it is no less a law, and ought to be acted on by honest governments. It is, at the same time, a salutary curb on the spirit of war and indebtment, which, since the modern theory of the perpetuation of debt, has drenched the earth with blood, and crushed its inhabitants under burthens ever accumulating. Had this principle been declared in the British bill of rights, England would have been placed under the happy disability of waging eternal war, and of contracting her thousand millions of public debt. In seeking then, for an ultimate term for the redemption of our debts, let us rally to this principle, and provide for their payment within the term of nineteen years at the farthest.[365]

Well Mr. Jefferson, not to argue, but having a perpetually debt, maybe you have a rolling generation agreeing with the debt. As the debt comes on, you have those who are alive

---

[365] To Wayles Eppes #2012 (M., June 1813.)

today, or their representatives agreeing to the debt, and those who have died off not worrying about it.

As the doctrine is that a public debt is a public blessing, so they think a perpetual one is a perpetual blessing, and therefore wish to make it so large that we can never pay it off.[366]

Some think that the United States should just write the debt off, and start over.

I am anxious about everything which may affect our credit. My wish would be to possess it in the highest degree, but to use it little. Were we without credit, we might be crushed by a nation of much inferior resources, but possessing higher credit.[367]

I told the President all that was ever necessary to establish our credit, was an efficient government, and an honest one, declaring it would sacredly pay our debts, laying taxes for this purpose and applying them to it.[368]

Mr. Jefferson, I believe the United States debt per capita is a little over sixty thousand dollars per person, man, woman and child. I doubt that they include the millions of illegals in the United States as part of that amount.

The honest payment of our debts, I deem [one of the] essential principles of our government and,

---

[366] To Nicholas Lewis #2067 (Pa., April 1792.)
[367] To General Washington #1920 (P-, 1788.)
[368] The Anas #1906 (Oct. 1792.)

consequently, [one] which ought to shape its admin-istration.[369]

It is a wise rule, and should be a fundamental in a government disposed to cherish its credit, and at the same time to restrain the use of it within the limits of its faculties, "never to borrow a dollar without laying a tax in the same instant for paying the interest annually, and the principal within a given term; and to consider that tax as pledged to the creditors on the public faith."

On such a pledge as this, sacredly observed, a government may always command, on a reasonable interest, all the lendable money of their citizens, while the necessity of an equivalent tax is a salutary warning to them and their constituents against op-pressions, bankruptcy, and its inevitable consequence, revolution. But the term of redemption must be moderate, and at any rate within the limit of their rightful powers. But what limits, it will be asked, does this prescribe to their powers? What is to hinder them from creating a perpetual debt? The laws of nature, I answer. The earth belongs to the living, not to the dead. The will and the power of man expire with his life, by nature's law.[370]

We are ruined if we do not overrule the principles that "the more we owe, the more prosperous we shall be"; "that a public debt furnishes the means of enterprise";

---

[369] First Inaugural Address #2063 (1801.)
[370] To John W. Eppes #1919 (M., June 1813.)

"that if ours should be once paid off, we should incur another by any means however extravagant."[371]

I think it hurts our citizens in ways other than just having a debt. For the last several years, interest rates have been nearly zero so the government may borrow at cheaper rates. It has been a serious hardship for families. Someone having saved $100,000 for retirement, getting 5% interest on their money, had $5,000 a year to spend in retirement. With the zero percent interest for the last 8 years, the individual may have spent the $5,000 from the principle to live, leaving now $60,000 principal. If interest rates were to magically raise to 5% again, there would only be $3000 a year to assist living on. As a large debtor, is the government keeping the interest rate low?

It is incumbent on every generation to pay its own debts as it goes. A principle which, if acted on, would save one-half the wars of the world.[372]

To preserve our independence, we must not let our rulers load us with perpetual debt. We must make our election between economy and liberty, or profusion and servitude.[373]

You do believe the United States should have credit, and the ability to borrow if needed?

Though much an enemy to the system of borrowing, yet I feel strongly the necessity of preserving the power to borrow. Without this we might be over-

---

[371] To James Monroe #2068 (Pa., 1791.)
[372] To Destutt Tracy #2002 (M., 1820.)
[373] To Samuel Kerchival #2056 (M., 1816.)

whelmed by another nation, merely by the force of its credit.[374]

I once thought that in the event of a war we should be obliged to suspend paying the interest of the public debt. But a dozen years more of experience and observation on our people and government, have satisfied me it will never be done. The sense of the necessity of public credit is so universal and so deeply rooted, that no other necessity will prevail against it.[375]

Over the years, since you were President, if the nation did not pay interest during a time of war, there would have been only fifteen to twenty years when the United States would have paid interest.

No man is more ardently intent to see the public debt soon and sacredly paid off than I am. This exactly marks the difference between Colonel Hamilton's views and mine, that I would wish the debt paid tomorrow; he wishes it never to be paid, but always to be a thing wherewith to corrupt and manage the Legislature.[376]

Our government has not, as yet, begun to act on the rule of loans and taxation going hand in hand. Had any loan taken place in my time, I should have strongly urged a redeeming tax. For the loan which has been made since the last session of Congress, we

[374] To The Treasury Commissioners #4785 (P., 1788.)
[375] To William Short #2057 (M., Nov.1814.)
[376] To President Washington #2061 (M., 1792.)

should now set the example of appropriating some particular tax, sufficient to pay the interest annually, and the principal within a fixed term, less than nineteen years. I hope yourself and your committee will render the immortal service of introducing this practice.[377]

There is still hope that someday Congress will pay attention to what they are doing and get control of this problem. Perhaps if Congressmen would think for themselves, in doing what they know is right, instead of following the leadership and the President.

---

[377] To John W. Eppes #4787 (M., June 1813.)

ON TAXATION

The increase of expense beyond income is an indication soliciting the employment of the pruning knife.[378]

We now get into the subject of paying our expenses and our debts, Mr. Jefferson. We are using the necessary word, taxation.

Government thinks that there is no limit in taking from the working class. Something happening now, is the government spending way beyond the citizen's means to pay, and yet not cutting our budget of unnecessary expenses. We do need a pruning in government.

I thought at first that the power of taxation [given in the new Federal Constitution] might have been limited. A little reflection soon convinced me it ought not to be.[379]

---

[378] To Spencer Roane #2849 (M., 1821.)
[379] To F. Hopkinson #8292 (P., March 1789.)

I know you first questioned the need of the Federal Government having a direct tax. Why did you come back with the idea the Federal Government should not be limited?

War requires every resource of taxation and credit.[380] *Calculation has convinced me that circumstances may arise, and probably will arise, wherein all the resources of taxation will be necessary for the safety of the State.*[381]

So you are looking at taxation as an emergency necessity rather than as a way to equalize everyone's wealth and stature.

I like the power given the Legislature [in the Federal Constitution] to levy taxes, and for that reason solely approve of the greater House being chosen by the people directly. For though I think a House chosen by them will be very illy qualified to legislate for the Union, for foreign nations, &c., yet this evil does not weigh against the good of preserving inviolate the fundamental principle that the people are not to be taxed but by representatives chosen immediately by themselves.[382]

This has not held back spending. Our debt keeps rising, and now, with our debt doubling over the last eight years, I would think we have to cut much expense.

The principle of the present majority is excessive expense, money enough to fill all their maws, or it will

---

[380] To General Washington #8322 (P., 1788.)
[381] To General Washington #8323 (P., Dec. 1788.)
[382] To James Madison #1594 (P., 1787.)

not be worth the risk of their supporting. * * * Paper money would be perilous even to the paper men. Nothing then but excessive taxation can get us along; and this will carry reason and reflection to every man's door, and particularly in the hour of election.[383]

How true you are. There has been no reason or reflection in how the people's money is used. We have a problem of social engineering with our tax dollars. The Democrats think they can equalize everybody.

I am conscious that an equal division of property is impracticable. But the consequences of this enormous inequality [in France] producing so much misery to the bulk of mankind, legislators cannot invent too many devices for subdividing property, only taking care to let their subdivisions go hand in hand with the natural affections of the human mind.[384]

One method you chose of making money less concentrated was ridding the United States of the law of primogeniture, whereby, the first born inherits all the wealth. Primogeniture was the reason my grandmother came from Denmark as a child. She said being the oldest, and a girl, she was just glad she was not killed so her brother would be the oldest. Being shipped to America, got rid of her.

The descent of property of every kind to all the children, or to all the brothers and sisters, or other

---

[383] To John Taylor #8310 (M., 1798.)
[384] Rev. James Madison #7030 (P., 1785.)

relations, in equal degree, is a politic measure, and a practicable one.[385]

Another means of silently lessening the inequality of property is to exempt all from taxation below a certain point, and to tax the higher portions of property in geometrical progression as they rise.[386]

We are doing that, the upper one percent in the nation pays nearly half of the federal income taxes, with the bottom sixty percent paying two percent.[387] But you are not, Mr. Jefferson, for taking wealth from someone, to equalize them with others lacking the wealth?

*Our wish is that * * * [there be] maintained that state of property, equal or unequal, which results to every man from his own industry, or that of his fathers.*[388]

Well let's talk taxes Mr. Jefferson. The cry "taxation without representation" was one of the reasons of the Revolutionary War and the break from England. Yet I believe we are in worse shape now, because Congress and the President have a new cry, "the joy of spending." Do they represent us, I could question it? Can you imagine the Federal Government spending $3.1 billion on workers placed on administrative leave; giving bonuses to DEA employees caught patronizing prostitutes; $150,000 to understand why politics stress us out; $65,473 to figure out what bugs do near a lightbulb;[389]

[385] Rev. James Madison #7029 (P., 1785.)
[386] Rev. James Madison #7038 (P., 1785.)
[387] Robert Frank, CNBC 14 Apr. 2015 http://www.cnbc.com/2015/04/13/top-1-pay-nearly-half-of-federal-income-taxes.html
[388] Second Inaugural Address (1805.)
[389] Jillian Kay Melchior, National Review, 02 Dec 2015

$545,000 for training courses for State Department officials to go before Congressional hearing?[390] This is power and spending gone wild. I am sure if this were money from their own pockets, it would not be spent in this ridiculous way.

The same prudence, which, in private life, would forbid our paying our money for unexplained projects, forbids it in the disposition of the public moneys.[391]

Shouldn't there be a check to stop such waste if they are incapable of representing the citizens? Maybe a balanced budget amendment would stop some of this nonsense.

*If there be anything amiss in the present state of our affairs, as the formidable deficit lately unfolded to us indicates, I ascribe it to the inattention of Congress to their duties, to their unwise dissipation and waste of the public contributions. They seemed, some little while ago, to be at a loss for objects whereon to throw away the supposed fathomless funds of the treasury. * * * I am aware that in one of their most ruinous vagaries the people were themselves betrayed into the same phrenzy with their representatives. The deficit produced, and a heavy tax to supply it, will, I trust, bring both to their sober senses.[392]*

As you know the wastes go on and on because Congressman are told to vote for a budget by their leaders, period. So we

http://www.nationalreview.com/article/427891/top-10-wasteful-government-expenses
[390] Federal Fumbles, Senator James Lankford
https://www.lankford.senate.gov/imo/media/doc/Federal_Fumbles_2015.pdf
[391] To Shelton Gilliam #2356 (W., 1808.)
[392] To Thomas Ritchie #8358 (M., 1820.)

have the waste of tax dollars to create a job for someone. You would think they would have heard of "Just say NO!"

We do not mean that our people shall be burdened with oppressive taxes to provide sinecures for the idle or the wicked, under color of providing for a civil list.[393]

Congress, President Obama, send me some money! We all know bugs are tempted by peer pressure to see how close they can go without getting burned. And why politics stresses us out, it is because of robo-calls and untruths (it is bad to say lies, might hurt someone's feelings). That is $215,000 I could have saved the American citizens. Sorry Mr. Jefferson, I went on a little tirade. I think most of us are feeling this way in the United States. Frustrated and angry, and it goes back to Congress. You make the appropriations, stop wasting American's money! You will get voted back in if you do right by your districts.

If we run into such debts, as that we must be taxed in our meat and in our drink, in our necessaries and our comforts, in our labors and our amusements, for our callings and our creeds, as the people of England are, our people, like them, must come to labor sixteen hours in the twenty-four, give the earnings of fifteen of these to the government for their debts and daily expenses; and the sixteenth being insufficient to afford us bread, we must live, as they now do, on oatmeal and potatoes; have no time to think, no means of calling the mismanagers to account; but be glad to

---

[393] Reply to Lord North's Proposition #7908 (July 1775.)

*obtain subsistence by hiring ourselves to rivet their chains on the necks of our fellow-sufferers. * * * And this is the tendency of all human governments.*

There is a lack of common sense. Congress has lost track of who they are and who they work for, and why they are in government.

A departure from principle in one instance becomes a precedent for a second; that second for a third; and so on, till the bulk of the society is reduced to be mere automatons of misery, to have no sensibilities left but for sinning and suffering.

Then begins, indeed, the bellum omnium in omnia [war of all against all], which some philosophers observing to be so general in this world, have mistaken it for the natural instead of the abusive state of man. And the fore horse of this frightful team is public debt. Taxation follows that, and in its train wretchedness and oppression.[394]

We are under a taxation bubble Mr. Jefferson! Our economy is suffering, because of a big failure of government to let the people, the markets, and a free economy, make life better for America. Government officials should look back in history to see how our economy grew from free enterprise, and then compare it to the socialist countries.

The American mind is now in that state of fever which the world has so often seen in the history of

---

[394] To Samuel Kerchival # 8302 (M., 1816.)

other nations. We are under the bank bubble, as England was under the South Sea bubble, France under the Mississippi bubble, and as every nation is liable to be, under whatever bubble, design, or delusion may puff up in moments when off their guard.[395]

Taxation is the most difficult function of government, and that against which their citizens are most apt to be refractory. The general aim is, therefore, to adopt the mode most consonant with the circumstances and sentiments of the country.[396]

Americans do not mind paying taxes if the taxes are fair and spent wisely. Communities often vote for and renew taxes when the citizens see that the money is being spent where promised and are reasonable.

The purse of the people is the real seat of sensibility. It is to be drawn upon largely, and they will then listen to truths which could not excite them through any other organ.[397]

Of the modes which are within the limits of right, that of raising within the year its whole expenses by taxation, might be beyond the abilities of our citizens to bear. It is, moreover, generally desirable that the public contribution should be as uniform as practicable from year to year, that our habits of industry and expense may become adapted to them; and that they

---

[395] To Charles Yancey #965 (M., Jan. 1816.)
[396] Preface to Tracy's Political Economy # 8311 (1816.)
[397] To A. H. Rowan #8312 (M., 1798.)

may be duly digested and incorporated with our annual economy.

This would keep our taxes and the governments expenses in line. The common person sees this, as they have to watch their spending The trouble is, Mr. Greed steps in and overtakes the elected officials, to a point the officials believe they are entitled to our earnings.

There remains, then, for us but the method of limited anticipation, the laying taxes for a term of years within that of our right, which may be sold for a present sum equal to the expenses of the year; in other words, to obtain a loan equal to the expenses of the year, laying a tax adequate to its interest, and to such a surplus as will reimburse, by growing instalments, the whole principle within the term. This is, in fact, what has been called raising money on the sale of annuities for years.

Paying for a program as you go, what a novel idea for our government. How about a balanced budget amendment to also help keep them in line. It is common sense, live within your means!

In this way a new loan, and of course a new tax, is requisite every year during the continuance of the war; and should that be so long as to produce an accumulation of tax beyond our ability, in time of war the resource would be an enactment of the taxes requisite to ensure good terms, by securing the lender, with a suspension of the payment of instalments of principal and perhaps of interest also, until the resto-ration of peace.

This method of anticipating our taxes, or of borrow-ing on annuities for years, insures repayment to the lender, guards the rights of posterity, prevents a perpetual alienation of the public contributions, and consequent destitution of every resource even for the ordinary support of government.[398]

What gets us excited Mr. Jefferson, is not the need for taxa-tion, it is because of the waste. All of our Congressmen tell us that they had to vote for the budget or close the govern-ment. So? They have the President giving them his proposed budget first. Why, because he might veto Congresses budget? So? Repeal the Budget and Accounting Act of 1921, and do your job. Present what Congress wants to fund. It is in the Constitution. "No money shall be drawn from the Treasury, but in Consequence of Appropriations made by Law; and a regular Statement and Account of Receipts and Expenditures of all public Money shall be published from time to time." Do the nose test, if you think it stinks, for sure it does. That is why we elect representatives. If the President wants to shut down government, that's on him. Oh my Mr. Jefferson, I can see how people can get worked up to Revolution as you did. America should have learned from the past, yet it is happen-ing again. Oh, I forgot, history is not being taught in government schools, so people do not know what has hap-pened and what their rights are.

---

[398] To J. W. Eppes #8321 (P.F., Sep. 1813.)

So inscrutable is the arrangement of causes and consequences in this world, that a two-penny duty on tea, unjustly imposed in a sequestered part of it, changes the condition of all its inhabitants.[399]

Sometimes a little thing like a two-penny tax is the breaking point of the citizens. It was in your time. I think the United States is near that now.

*It behooves us to avail ourselves of every occasion * * * for taking off the surcharge [of offices and expense] that it may never be seen here that, after leaving to labor the smallest portion of its earnings on which it can subsist, government shall itself consume the residue of what it was instituted to guard.*[400]

Yes it does, our government is fat, and the trimming of it will help every American. The trimming needs to happen at every level of government, but the further up the chain from local you go, the fatter it gets.

The taxes with which we are familiar, class themselves readily according to the basis on which they rest. 1. Capital. 2. Income. 3. Consumption. These may be considered as commensurate; Consumption being generally equal to Income, and Income the annual profit of Capital.

A government may select any one of these bases for the establishment of its system of taxation, and so frame it as to reach the faculties of every member of

---

[399] Autobiography #7618 (1821.)
[400] First Annual Message #4308 (Dec. 1801.)

the society, and to draw from him his equal propor-
tion of the public contributions; and, if this be correct-
ly obtained, it is the perfection of the function of tax-
ation. But, when once a government has assumed its
basis, to select and tax special articles from either of
the other classes, is double taxation.

For example, if the system be established on the basis
of Income, and his just proportion on that scale has
been already drawn from every one, to step into the
field of Consumption, and tax special articles in that,
as broadcloth or homespun, wine or whiskey, a coach
or a wagon, is doubly taxing the same article. For
that portion of Income with which these articles are
purchased, having already paid its tax as Income, to
pay another tax on the thing it purchased, is paying
twice for the same thing, it is an aggrievance on the
citizens who use these articles in exoneration of those
who do not, contrary to the most sacred of the duties
of a government, to do equal and impartial justice to
all its citizens.

So the United States has an income tax. Missouri has an
income tax. It also has a sales tax. You are saying it is double
taxation on the part of Missouri to tax my income and then
to tax the sale of my book. Excise taxes on the federal level
are all double taxation, as we have a national income tax. We
have excise taxes on fuel, tobacco, firearms, gambling, tires,
the list goes on and on. Look at your phone bill, until 2006,
we still had an excise tax on our phones for the Spanish
American War. Then the states also get in on the act. Missouri has a $0.17 tax on a pack of cigarettes, while New

York's is $4.35 a pack. That is why there are signs about bootlegging cigarettes along the interstates. Why do we need all of these different taxes? Is it to help the illegal bootleggers, somebodies brother in law? Makes me wonder, is the Government trying to make criminals?

Taxes should be continued by annual or biennial reenactments, because a constant hold, by the nation, of the strings of the public purse, is a salutary restraint from which an honest government ought not to wish, nor a corrupt one to be permitted to be free.[401]

How far it may be the interest and the duty of all to submit to this sacrifice on other grounds; for instance, to pay for a time an impost on the importation of certain articles, in order to encourage their manufacture at home, or an excise on others injurious to the morals or health of the citizens, will depend on a series of considerations of another order, and beyond the proper limits of this note.

I think the governments need to decide on what is important based on their constituency, fund those items and stop the other programs, based on their ability to pay for them and to pay down the debt. If private industry is developing a bug free light, or a "save the bug" cool light, they will fund a study if it is necessary to sell a new product. Government does not need to run all things, including our lives. They should stick to their function and let private industry and individuals run themselves. It will improve the economy.

---

[401] To J. W. Eppes #8348 (P.F., Sep. 1813.)

*** *To this a single observation shall yet be added. Whether property alone, and the whole of what each citizen possesses, shall be subject to contribution, or only its surplus after satisfying his first wants, or whether the faculties of body and mind shall contribute also from their annual earnings, is a question to be decided. But, when decided, and the principle settled, it is to be equally and fairly applied to all. To take from one, because it is thought that his own industry and that of his fathers has acquired too much, in order to spare to others, who, or whose fathers have not exercised equal industry and skill, is to violate arbitrarily the first principle of association, "the guarantee to every one of a free exercise of his industry, and the fruits acquired by it". If the overgrown wealth of an individual be deemed dangerous to the State, the best corrective is the law of equal inheritance to all in equal degree; and the better, as this enforces a law of nature, while extra-taxation violates it.*[402]

Why not the "Fair Tax," for America! The Fair Tax is a consumption tax rather than an income tax. One tax for each level of government, and with that we can decide where we want to live. We see how individuals and businesses have been moving out of some of the high tax states and cities, the problem is that some of those leaving might have been also the cause of the higher taxes. States and cities should not be allowed to entice private business with tax dollars. We see it over and over again with sports stadiums. Teams leave the

---

[402] Note in Destutt Tracy's Political Economy #8279 (1816.)

city or state before the stadiums are even paid for. Tax In-
crement Financing (TIF's) are another way private business is
supported. If it makes sense to build a hotel or a mall, it will
happen. We have towns paying businesses, to move a few
miles down the road. This has to be stopped all across the
entire country in order for it to work.

*What more is necessary to make us a happy and
prosperous people? Still one thing more: a wise and
frugal Government, which shall restrain men from
injuring one another, which shall leave them otherwise free to regulate their own pursuits of industry
and improvement, and shall not take from the mouth
of labor the bread it has earned. This is the sum of
good government, and this is necessary to close the
circle of our felicities.[403]*

This is a government working for the people, power and
greed in check, so the economy can grow, creating jobs, salaries and new spending. This cycle grows the economy, and
yes, the government will also get more income, with either
more spending by the consumers or by more income of the
citizens, depending upon the tax. Life goes on, and is better.

*The powers of the government for the collection of
taxes are found to be perfect, so far as they have been
tried. This has been as yet only by duties on consumption. As these fall principally on the rich, it is a general desire to make them contribute the whole money
we want, if possible. And we have a hope that they
will furnish enough for the expenses of Government*

---

[403] First Inaugural Address #3315 (1801.)

and the interest of our whole public debt, foreign and domestic.[404]

In 1913 the United States started the income tax as a permanent, regular tax on the citizens. The Treasury Department's Tax code now consists of nearly 3000 pages, but it takes 75,000 pages to inform us how to pay our taxes. It is a joke, creating a large bureaucracy, to administer it. A tax should be simple, where even a Congressman can understand it.

*The objects of finance in the United States have hitherto been very simple; merely to provide for the support of the government on its peace establishment, and to pay the debt contracted * * *. The means provided for these objects were ample, and resting on a consumption which little affected the poor, may be said to have been felt by none.*[405]

Simple is good. The American citizens cannot learn the ever changing nonsense, authorized by Congress and administered by the Executive Department. The National Society of Accountants had a survey showing the average cost of professional tax preparation is $261. A simple non itemized 1040 Form averages $152.[406] That is just the cost to prepare the form for the government. Come on, so called government representatives! Represent the people who elected you, not the government bureaucracy! If the citizens have more of their own money, they can have businesses and hire displaced government workers. The time to start is now.

---

[404] To Comte de Moustier #8271 (Pa., 1790.)
[405] To J. W. Eppes #8332 (P.F., Sep. 1813.)
[406] https://www.irs.com/articles/tax-preparation-costs-and-fees

The maxim of buying nothing without the money in our pockets to pay for it, would make of our country one of the happiest on earth. Experience during the war proved this; and I think every man will remember, that under all the privations it obliged him to submit to during that period, he slept sounder, and awoke happier than he can do now.[407]

Avoiding debt is good. A balanced budget should be required. Mr. Jefferson, we have all sorts of weird taxes for social engineering. What do you think of cities, taxing things like soda pop and other junk food?

Taste cannot be controlled by law.[408]

What about luxury taxes on things like yachts, expensive cars, and jewelry? President George H. W. Bush tried to have one but it failed to raise the money, and damaged the businesses and individuals who worked in the business.

The government which steps out of the ranks of the ordinary articles of consumption to select and lay under disproportionate burdens a particular one, because it is a comfort, pleasing to the taste, or necessary to the health, and will, therefore, be bought, is, in that particular, a tyranny.[409]

Sound principles will not justify our taxing the industry of our fellow citizens to accumulate treasure for wars to happen we know not when, and which might

---

[407] To A. Donald #1995 (P., 1787.)
[408] Notes on a Money Unit #8278 (1784.)
[409] To Samuel Smith #8300 (M., 1823.)

not perhaps happen but from the temptations offered by that treasure.[410] It is [the people's] sweat which is to earn all the expenses of the war, and their blood which is to flow in expiation of the causes of it.[411]

It sounds like you are sympathetic to the American worker, Mr. Jefferson. I do not think we need to worry about building a war chest, as I doubt our debt will ever end.

We have an Inheritance Tax in the United States of nearly forty percent, and also a tax on gifts to others. Are you seeing a pattern that our monies are being taxed over and over again.

If the overgrown wealth of an individual be deemed dangerous to the State, the best corrective is the law of equal inheritance to all in equal degree; and the better, as this enforces a law of nature, while extra taxation violates it.[412] The General Government is incompetent to legislate on the subject of inheritances.[413]

Thank you for repeating that. If it is said enough, maybe someone will listen.

---

[410] First Annual Message #8242 (1801.)
[411] To Elbridge Gerry #4317 (Pa., 1799.)
[412] Note to Tracy's Political Economy #3963 (1816.)
[413] To President Washington #3965 (1792.)

ON RELIGION

I believe, with the Quaker preacher, that he who steadily observes those moral precepts in which all religions concur, will never be questioned, at the gates of heaven, as to the dogmas in which they all differ. That on entering there, all these are left behind us, and the * * * Presbyterians and Papists, will find themselves united in all principles which are in concert with the reason of the supreme mind. Of all the systems of morality antient or modern, which have come under my observation, none appear to me so pure as that of Jesus. He who follows this steadily need not, I think, be uneasy, altho' he cannot comprehend the subtleties & mysteries erected on his doctrines by those who, calling themselves his special followers & favorites, would make him come into the world to lay snares for all understandings but theirs. * * * In all essential points, you and I are of the same *religion; and I am too old to go into enquiries & changes as to the unessential.* [414]

The eyes of the virtuous all over the earth are turned with anxiety on us as the only depositaries of the sacred fire of liberty. [415]

All the nations of the earth see our liberty. Many desire to live here, and others desire to destroy our liberty. The one thing they all desire is the money that the liberty, education, and labor has created.

*Among the most inestimable of our blessings is that * * * of liberty to worship our Creator in the way we think most agreeable to His will; a liberty deemed in other countries incompatible with good government and yet proved by our experience to be its best support.* [416]

So you are saying religion is the best support of good government. Could I imply that the lack of religion produces not so good government?

It shows how necessary was the care of the Creator in making the moral principle so much a part of our constitution as that no errors of reasoning or of speculation might lead us astray from its observance in practice. [417] *Moral duties are as obligatory on nations as on individuals.* [418]

[414] Thomas Jefferson to William Canby, LOC, September 18, 1813
http://hdl.loc.gov/loc.mss/mtj.mtjbib021517
[415] To John Hollins #8710 (M., 1811.)
[416] Reply to Baptist Address #7232 (1807.)
[417] To Thomas Law #5523 (M., 1814.)
[418] The Anas #5537 (1808.)

There never was a more pure and sublime system of morality delivered to man than is to be found in the four Evangelists.[419]

We now have leaders in our nation who are considering their own interests, or the interests of the party, rather than the interest of the United States. Morality has fallen on the wayside as many consider it religion.

Self-interest, or rather self-love, or egoism, has been more plausibly substituted as the basis of morality. But I consider our relations with others as constituting the boundaries of morality. With ourselves we stand on the ground of identity, not of relation, which last, requiring two subjects, excludes self-love confined to a single one. To ourselves, in strict language, we can owe no duties, obligation requiring also two parties. Self-love, therefore, is no part of morality.

Hillary Clinton, former Secretary of State, is a prime example of a leader whose self interest in having a server in her home so she could control who sees her emails was more important than the security of our nation's secrets. She exposed our secrets and lied to the American people about it.

Indeed it is exactly its counterpart. It is the sole antagonist of virtue, leading us constantly by our propensities to self-gratification in violation of our moral duties to others. Accordingly, it is against this enemy that are erected the batteries of moralists and religionists, as the only obstacle to the practice of morality.

---

[419] To Samuel Greenhow #5531 (M., 1814.)

Take from man his selfish propensities, and he can have nothing to seduce him from the practice of virtue. Or subdue those propensities by education, instruction, or restraint, and virtue remains without a competitor.[420]

I know the Founding Fathers figured in religion as the basis of our constitution and the nation's morality. Did you figure it would last?

It was not expected in this age, that nations so honorably distinguished by their advances in science and civilization, would suddenly cast away the esteem they had merited from the world, and, revolting from the empire of morality, assume a character in history, which all the tears of their posterity will never wash from its pages.[421]

As you travelled about, it was a slower time. Did you have time to consider and formulate your beliefs?

Reading, reflection and time have convinced me that the interests of society require the observation of those moral precepts only in which all religions agree (for all forbid us to steal, murder, plunder, or bear false witness), and that we should not intermeddle with the particular dogmas in which all religions differ, and which are totally unconnected with morality. In all of them we see good men, and as many in one as another.

---

420 To Thomas Law #5526 (M., 1814.)
421 Reply to Address #5533 (1808.)

The varieties in the structure and action of the human mind as in those of the body, are the work of our Creator, against which it cannot be a religious duty to erect the standard of uniformity. The practice of morality being necessary for the wellbeing of society, he has taken care to impress its precepts so indelibly on our hearts that they shall not be effaced by the subtleties of our brain. We all agree in the obligation of the moral precepts of Jesus, and nowhere will they be found delivered in greater purity than in His discourses. It is, then, a matter of principle with me to avoid disturbing the tranquillity of others by the expression of any opinion on the innocent questions on which we schismatize.[422]

This is true of a Christian sense. Most Christian sects have the same fundamentals.

*Almighty God hath created the mind free, and manifested His supreme will that free it shall remain by making it altogether insusceptible of restraint. * * * All attempts to influence it by temporal punishments or burthens, or by civil incapacitations, tend only to beget habits of hypocrisy and meanness, and are a departure from the plan of the Holy Author of our religion, who, being Lord both of body and mind, yet chose not to propagate it by coercions on either, as was in his Almighty power to do, but to exalt it by its influence on reason alone.*[423]

---

[422] To James Fishback #5529 (M., 1809.)
[423] Statute of Religious Freedom #7226 (1779.)

The free will that God has created, Mr. Jefferson, gives many Americans hope, that the country may be turned around from the political correctness, that seeks to destroy our freedoms. As we move through the Revolution of 2016, many are in hopes that our nation will get ahold of its finances, and get them under control. They are in hopes that they will get their religious freedom back; they are in hopes of getting their state's rights back; and they are in hopes of getting their Constitution back. For some who call you an atheist, as a way of discrediting you, it seems that you call on the Almighty often.

I do not wish to trouble the world with my creed, nor to be troubled for them. These accounts are to be settled only with Him who made us; and to Him we leave it, with charity for all others, of whom, also, He is the only rightful and competent judge.[424]

Mr. Jefferson, there are several issues pressing in the United States, that I would like to ask you about. Some we may have touched on, but desire more. You wrote of a "wall of separation" between church and state, that the Supreme Court has chosen to use in their defense of removing religion from everything.

Believing that religion is a matter which lies solely between man and his God, that he owes account to none other for his faith or his worship, that the legislative powers of government reach actions only, and not opinions, I contemplate with sovereign reverence that act of the whole American people which declared that their Legislature should "make no law respecting

---

[424] To Timothy Pickering #7250 (M., 1821.)

an establishment of religion, or prohibiting the free exercise thereof", thus building a wall of separation between Church and State.[425]

I always took this as not having an official church for the nation and that they would not tax people in support of that church.

I am for freedom of religion, and against all manoeuvres to bring about a legal ascendancy of one sect over another.[426] No provision in our Constitution ought to be dearer to man than that which protects the rights of conscience against the enterprises of the civil authority. It has not left the religion of its citizens under the power of its public functionaries, were it possible that any of these should consider a conquest over the conscience of men either attainable or applicable to any desirable purpose.[427]

The courts however, on each new case, takes more away from the people. The Supreme Court took prayer from schools, then even from graduations. Monsignor Kurwicki, pastor of the Cathedral of Jefferson City and the Chaplain for the Missouri House of Representatives, a fellow collector of books on history, laughs, "Ha! Ha! As long as they have tests in schools, there will be prayer in schools." Now, prayer before a public body is questioned, as well as the Ten Commandments being on a rock. And then there is our tax dollars for abortion. The courts blame you for a "high and impregnable" wall between church and State.

---

[425] To Danbury Baptists #1269 (1802.)
[426] To Elbridge Gerry #7230 (Pa., 1799.)
[427] To New London Methodists #1629 (1809.)

*One of the amendments to the Constitution * * * expressly declares, that "Congress shall make no law respecting an establishment of religion, or prohibiting the free exercise thereof, or abridging the freedom of speech, or of the press"; thereby guarding in the same sentence, and under the same words, the freedom of religion, of speech, and of the press; insomuch, that whatever violates either, throws down the sanctuary which covers the others.*[428]

Unfortunately there is the Johnson Amendment in the tax code that was passed in 1954, named for Lyndon Johnson, a Democrat who later became President. It limits supporting, opposing or speaking on political matters in the church. It threatens churches of losing their tax exempt status. I believe it to be unconstitutional.

I consider the government of the United States as interdicted by the Constitution from intermeddling with religious institutions, their doctrines, discipline, or exercises. This results not only from the provision that no law shall be made respecting the establishment or free exercise of religion, but from that also which reserves to the States the powers not delegated to the United States. Certainly, no power to prescribe any religious exercise, or to assume any authority in religious discipline, has been delegated to the General Government. It must then rest with the States, as far as it can be in any human authority.[429]

---

[428] Kentucky Resolutions #3231 (1798.)
[429] To Rev. Samuel Miller #7219 (W., 1808.)

It is amazing Mr. Jefferson, that President James Madison, considered the writer of the Constitution and Bill of Rights and you, as President, regularly attended church services in the House of Representatives. The Gospel was also preached in the Supreme Court Chambers and other executive branch buildings. In an article on Religion and the Founding of the American Republic, the Library of Congress site provides:

"Jefferson's actions may seem surprising because his attitude toward the relation between religion and government is usually thought to have been embodied in his recommendation that there exist "a wall of separation between church and state." In that statement, Jefferson was apparently declaring his opposition, as Madison had done in introducing the Bill of Rights, to a "national" religion. In attending church services on public property, Jefferson and Madison consciously and deliberately were offering symbolic support to religion as a prop for republican government."[430]

It once again looks like all you wanted to do was not have a national religion, and not to tax the citizens to support the church. It is unfortunate that the Supreme Court has twisted, this one clause "wall of separation", from one of your letters, into the abomination that they have. Haven't they heard about actions being louder than words.

In matters of religion, I have considered that its free exercise is placed by the Constitution independent of the powers of the General Government. I have, therefore, undertaken, on no occasion, to prescribe the religious exercises suited to it; but have left them, as

[430] https://www.loc.gov/exhibits/religion/rel06-2.html

the Constitution found them, under the direction and discipline of State or church authorities acknowledged by the several religious societies.[431]

You have followed the Constitution, and had religious services in the Capitol and the Supreme Court. Duh! Are Supreme Court judges stupid or something? Oh yes, I forgot, four letter curse words are okay, but "stupid" should not be said. Might hurt somebody's feelings.

The Constitution leaves the churches free, and does not force the beliefs of one sect upon another.

Is uniformity attainable? Millions of innocent men, women and children, since the introduction of Christianity, have been burnt, tortured, fined and imprisoned; yet we have not advanced one inch towards uniformity.[432]

Unfortunately the burning, the torturing, the fining and imprisonment is going on in many parts of the world. It is not happening in the United States, at least not yet.

*We have solved * * *, the great and interesting question whether freedom of religion is compatible with order in government, and obedience to the laws. And we have experienced the quiet as well as the comfort which results from leaving every one to profess freely and openly those principles of religion which are the*

---

[431] Second Inaugural Address #7218 (1805.)
[432] Notes on Religion #8649 (1782.)

inductions of his own reason, and the serious convictions of his own inquiries.[433]

The Supreme Court may not agree with you.

The Constitution has not placed our religious rights under the power of any public functionary.[434]

No man complains of his neighbor for ill management of his affairs, for an error in sowing his land, or marrying his daughter, for consuming his substance in taverns, pulling down, building, &c. In all these he has his liberty: but if he do not frequent the church, or there conform to ceremonies, there is an immediate uproar. The care of every man's soul belongs to himself. But what if he neglect the care of it? Well, what if he neglect the care of his health or estate, which more nearly relate to the State? Will the magistrate make a law that he shall not be poor or sick? Laws provide against injury from others, but not from ourselves. God Himself will not save men against their wills.[435]

This is true, the government does not force anyone to do or not do in the name of religion. It did not force anyone to say a prayer in Congress or in a public school. It seems some do want the government to "outlaw" poverty and bad health. This is how liberty is lost incrementally, to the "Nanny State."

No man has power to let another prescribe his faith.

---

[433] Reply to Virginia Baptists #7233 (1801.)
[434] To Pittsburg Methodists #7235 (1808.)
[435] Notes on Religion #7240 (1776?)

Faith is not faith without believing.[436]

Many say, you, Thomas Jefferson are a Deist or an Atheist. I know you do not like labels, especially in regard to religion, but what would you call yourself?

To the corruptions of Christianity I am indeed, opposed; but not to the genuine precepts of Jesus himself. I am a Christian, in the only sense in which he wished any one to be; sincerely attached to his doctrines, in preference to all others; ascribing to himself every human excellence; and believing he never claimed any other.[437]

Can the liberties of a nation be thought secure when we have removed their only firm basis, a conviction in the minds of the people that these liberties are of the gift of God? That they are not to be violated but with his wrath? Indeed, I tremble for my country when I reflect that God is just.[438]

---

[436] Notes on Religion #7216 (1776?)
[437] Thomas Jefferson to Benjamin Rush, LOC, April 21, 1803
http://hdl.loc.gov/loc.mss/mtj.mtjbib012336
[438] Notes on Virginia #7941 (1782.)

ON THE WAR ON TERROR

Truth and reason are eternal. They have prevailed. And they will eternally prevail, however, in times and places they may be overborne for a while by violence military, civil, or ecclesiastical.[439]

The President is Commander in Chief. You held that position. We are again at war in the Middle East, as you were with the Barbary Wars. There is a difference however in size and scope. It is also a war on terror against radical Islamic terrorists, both inside the United States and abroad. Some call it a religious war, as the foundation of it is in the Islamic religion. Do you recall the words of the Ambassador you told us earlier?

The Ambassador answered us that it was founded on the Laws of their Prophet, that it was written in their

---

[439] To Rev. Mr. Knox #8599 (M., 1810)

Koran, that all nations who should not have acknowledged their authority were sinners, that it was their right and duty to make war upon them wherever they could be found, and to make slaves of all they could take as Prisoners, and that every Musselman [Muslims] who should be slain in battle was sure to go to Paradise.[440]

Yes Mr. Jefferson, we, who are not Muslims, are sinners, and it is their right, according to them to make war on us and to make slaves of us. They talk good of us to get their way, but their religion allows them to lie to advance Islam.

* * * very early thought it would be best to effect a peace through the medium of war. * * * However, if it is decided that we shall buy a peace, I know no reason for delaying the operation, but should rather think it ought to be hastened; but I should prefer the obtaining it by war. 1. Justice is in favor of this opinion. 2. Honor favors it. 3. It will procure us respect in Europe; and respect is a safeguard to interest. 4. It will arm the Federal head with the safest of all the instruments of coercion over its delinquent members, and prevent it from using what would be less safe.[441]

The motives pleading for war rather than tribute [to the Muslim States] are numerous and honorable; those opposing them are mean and short-sighted.[442]

---

[440] T. Jefferson & J. Adams to John Jay, LOC, March 28, 1786
http://hdl.loc.gov/loc.mss/mtj.mtjbib001849
[441] To John Adams #752 (P., July 1786.)
[442] To James Monroe #770 (P., 1785.)

So war is preferred to safeguard our interests and our country?

Sole depositaries of the remains of human liberty, our duty to ourselves, to posterity, and to mankind, calls on us by every motive which is sacred or honorable, to watch over the safety of our beloved country during the troubles which agitate and convulse the residue of the world, and to sacrifice to that all personal and local considerations.[443]

Let's go a little further into what the Muslim religion allows. Muslim men can rape their slaves, American Christian women. It is allowed in the Koran and under Sharia law. Look what is going on in Europe. Nineteen Yazidis girls were burned alive in a cage, witnessed by hundreds, for not having sex with their captors in Mosul.[444] This is happening to Christians, Jews and other non-Muslim girls. America is next ladies if your elected leaders allow it. My lovely wife, Andrea said it will be the women, and the grace of God, who stop this in our country. I hope she is correct. Supposedly the defenders of women's rights, the Clintons, specifically former President Bill Clinton, was paid several million dollars by a company running sharia schools. The Bill, Hillary and Chelsea Clinton Foundation, the Clinton Foundation, for short, also received millions of dollars from the same company. Are the Clintons registered as foreign agents? Should they be?

The time to guard against corruption and tyranny is before they shall have gotten hold of us. It is better to

---

[443] To New York Legislature #8724 (1809.)
[444] http://www.christianpost.com/news/isis-horror-19-girls-burned-alive-iron-cage-refusing-sex-terror-group-164913/

keep the wolf out of the fold, than to trust to drawing his teeth and talons after he shall have entered.[445]

The beating and oppressing of women; cutting the hands off of thieves; the real thing of an eye for an eye, etc.; the " honor killing" of daughters who become westernized or dates an American boy; death, crucifixion, or multiple amputations for spreading corruption in the land; the execution of homosexuals; torture until death for turning from Islam; the stoning to death of adulterers; the whipping or caning of fornicators, gamblers, drinkers of alcohol and of drug users; and death for criticizing Muhammad, Islam or the Koran.

It is an obligation of every government to yield protection to its citizens as the consideration of their obedience.[446] *Rebellion to tyrants is obedience to God.*[447]

Islam is the supreme religion, as the Nazi's were the supreme race, according to them. Get rid of all in the way. Some say, that we have the westernized version of Islam. Sorry, but there is but one Islam, one Koran.

How far does the duty of toleration extend?

1. No church is bound by the duty of toleration to retain within her bosom obstinate offenders against her laws.

---

[445] Notes on Virginia #8637 (1782.)
[446] To John Jay #1294 (P., 1785.)
[447] Motto on Jefferson's Seal #8640

2. *We have no right to prejudice another in his civil enjoyments because he is of another church. If any man err from the right way, it is his own misfortune, no injury to thee; nor therefore art thou to punish him in the things of this life because thou supposeth he will be miserable in that which is to come on the contrary, according to the spirit of the gospel, charity, bounty, liberality are due him.[448]*

Whatsoever is lawful in the Commonwealth, or permitted to the subject in the ordinary way, cannot be forbidden to him for religious uses; and whatsoever is prejudicial to the Commonwealth in their ordinary uses and, therefore, prohibited by the laws, ought not to be permitted to churches in their sacred rites. For instance, it is unlawful in the ordinary course of things, or in a private house, to murder a child. It should not be permitted any sect then to sacrifice children: it is ordinarily lawful (or temporarily lawful) to kill calves or lambs. They may, therefore, be religiously sacrificed, but if the good of the State required a temporary suspension of killing lambs, as during a siege, sacrifices of them may then be rightfully suspended also. This is the true extent of toleration.[449]

So Mr. Jefferson, how far do we go with the idea of "freedom of religion." Do we go with the values of most of America, or a few of the liberal politicians and judges.

---

[448] Notes on Religion #7260 (1776?)
[449] Notes on Religion #7237 (1776?)

The question you propose, whether circumstances do not sometimes occur, which make it a duty in officers of high trust, to assume authorities beyond the law, is easy of solution in principle, but sometimes embarrassing in practice. A strict observance of the written laws is doubtless one of the high duties of a good citizen, but it is not the highest. The laws of necessity, of self-preservation, of saving our country when in danger, are of higher obligation. To lose our country by a scrupulous adherence to written law, would be to lose the law itself, with life, liberty, property, and all those who are enjoying them with us; thus absurdly sacrificing the end to the means.[450]

I hope our leaders understand that. We have Islamic sharia law creeping into America, we have terrorists killing Americans, and we have part of the country accepting and another not accepting that the religion and the actions are intertwined. Muslims take their actions from what they believe their religion states. Although this is the radical part of their religion, even making war on their own. Americans want to keep their country from being taken over from outsiders, who want to change our society, our laws, our Constitution, as has happened in Europe.

I know but one code of morality for men, whether acting singly or collectively. He who says I will be a rogue when I act in company with a hundred others, but an honest man when I act alone, will be believed in the former assertion, but not in the latter.[451] We

---

450 To J. B. Colvin #4528 (M., Sep. 1810.)
451 To James Madison #5521 (P., 1789.)

wish to preserve the morals of our citizens from being vitiated by courses of lawless plunder and murder.[452]

I consider Europe, at present, as a world apart from us, about which it is improper for us even to form opinions, or to indulge any wishes but the general one, that whatever is to take place in it, may be for its happiness.[453]

England voted to get out of the European Union. I believe that the European Union's open borders policies was a big factor. They have sharia law and courts in the European nations for Muslims. There are 88 in the United Kingdom and the Muslims are trying to replace common law. It is now slipping into the United States courts.

It is the right of every nation to prohibit acts of sovereignty from being exercised by any other within its limits.[454] *The declaration, that religious faith shall be unpunished, does not give impunity to criminal acts, dictated by religious error.*[455]

That is the key Mr. Jefferson, it does not give impunity to criminal acts, dictated by religious error. Sharia law cannot be allowed, not only by the courts, but also in the neighborhoods. Muslims want us to tolerate them using our laws, but they do not want to tolerate us and our laws.

---

[452] To George Hammond #5545 (Pa., 1793.)
[453] To Julian V. Niemcewiez #2774 (M., April 1807.)
[454] To E. C. Genet #5887 (Pa., June 1793.)
[455] To James Madison #817 (P., July 1788.)

If Muslims want to follow the full extent of their religion, they need to go where it is fully accepted. Instead of bringing Muslim refugees to the United States, we should help them get their territories back into a safe place to live. Most of the refugees would prefer to live in their own country, but because of danger of rape, abuse and death, they are escaping to save the lives of their children and themselves.

I have ever thought religion a concern purely between our God and our consciences, for which we were accountable to Him, and not to the priests. I never told my own religion, nor scrutinized that of another. I never attempted to make a convert nor wished to change another's creed. I have ever judged of the religion of others by their lives * * * for it is in our lives, and not from our words, that our religion must be read.[456]

Donald Trump got into the presidential race, and his initial support was on his immigration policy of keeping the illegals out of the country, sending the illegals who are in the country, home; and to close our borders to Muslims until the United States has a way to tell the friend from the enemy.

The resistance which our Republic has opposed to a course of operation, for which it was not destined, shows a strength of body which affords the most flattering presage of duration. I hope we shall now be permitted to steer her in her natural course, and to

---

[456] To Mrs. M. Harrison Smith #7249 (M., 1816.)

show by the smoothness of her motion the skill with which she has been formed for it.[457]

It has been peculiarly unfortunate for us, personally, that the portion in the history of mankind, at which we were called to take a share in the direction of their affairs, was such an one as history has never before presented. At any other period, the even-handed justice we have observed towards all nations, the efforts we have made to merit their esteem by every act which candor or liberality could exercise, would have preserved our peace, and secured the un-qualified confidence of all other nations in our faith and probity.

But the hurricane which is now blasting the world, physical and moral, has prostrated all the mounds of reason as well as right. All those calculations which, at any other period, would have been deemed honor-able, of the existence of a moral sense in man, indi-vidually or associated, of the connection which the laws of nature have established between his duties and his interests, of a regard for honest fame and the esteem of our fellow men, have been a matter of reproach on us, as evidences of imbecility.

Trump received millions of more votes, than the Republican Party has ever had in a primary.

It is the manners and spirit of a people which pre-serve a republic in vigor. A degeneracy in these is a

---

[457] To General Warren #7309 (W., March 1801.)

canker which soon eats to the heart of its laws and constitution.[458]

Hopefully, the excitement of the Revolution of 2016 will carry into the general election. The Democrats do not consider our open boarders as a security risk to the nation. The knowledge is out there that terrorists are coming into our country.

All the world is now politically mad. Men, women, children talk nothing else, and you know that naturally they talk much, loud and warm. Society is spoiled by it, at least for those who, like myself, are but lookers on. You, too, have had your political fever.[459]

I guess I have the fever, and I am not a twenty-four hour news junkie. People need to pay attention to what is happening to our country and the world.

*As if it could be a folly for an honest man to suppose that another could be honest also, when it is their interest to be so. And when is this state of things to end? The principle that force is right, is become the principle of the nation itself. They would not permit an honest minister, were accident to bring such an one into power, to relax their system of lawless * * *.*[460]

In the United States, 2015, we had 3.3 million Muslims.[461] A poll by the Polling Company for the Center for Security Policy

---

458 Notes on Virginia #6250 (1782.)
459 To Mrs. William Bingham #9169 (P., 1788.)
460 To Caesar A. Rodney #5534 (M., Feb. 1810.)
461 http://www.pewresearch.org/fact-tank/2016/01/06/a-new-estimate-of-the-u-s-muslim-population/

(CSP) shows more than half (51%) of U.S. Muslims polled believe either that they should have the choice of American or sharia courts, or that they should have their own tribunals to apply sharia. Only 39% of those polled said that Muslims in the U.S. should be subject to American courts.[462]

What has caused presidential candidate Trump to get his support, is his stance on controlling the borders, because that same poll shows that nearly one-fifth of Muslim respondents said that the use of violence in the United States is justified in order to make sharia the law of the land in this country.

Although our prospect is peace, our policy and purpose are to provide for defence by all those means to which our resources are competent.[463] Let common sense and common honesty have fair play and they will soon set things to rights.[464]

The Republicans are trying to get America back to a safe and moral place, where we may have life, liberty and the pursuit of happiness. The Democrats and presidential candidate Hillary Clinton want to bring more people into the United States for more Democrat votes, period. President Obama says the United States is not at war with Islam, but with people who have perverted the religion.

It would be a dangerous delusion were a confidence in the men of our choice to silence our fears for the safety

---

[462]http://www.centerforsecuritypolicy.org/2015/06/23/nationwide-poll-of-us-muslims-shows-thousands-support-shariah-jihad/

[463] To James Bowdoin #2141 (W., 1806.)

[464] To Ezra Stiles #3772 (P., 1786.)

of our rights.[465] *To save the Republic * * * is the first and supreme law.*[466] *An instant of delay in executive proceedings may be fatal to the whole nation.*[467]

Your ideas of the moral obligations of governments are perfectly correct. The man who is dishonest as a statesman would be a dishonest man in any station. It is strangely absurd to suppose that a million of human beings, collected together, are not under the same moral laws which bind each of them separately.[468]

I hope some means will turn up of reconciling our faith and honor with peace.[469] *I bless the Almighty Being, Who, in gathering together the waters under the heavens into one place, divided the dry land of your hemisphere from the dry lands of ours, and said, at least be there peace.*[470]

The oceans help, but we have the land to the North and South of us to worry about. We also have President Obama wanting to bring in refugees, with no vetting to see if they are terrorist or a true refugee. That is why developing a safe place for the refugees in their lands is so important.

Perhaps Congress, in the meantime, in their care for the safety of the citizen, as well as that for their own protection, may declare by law what is necessary and proper to enable them to carry into execution the

---

[465] Kentucky Resolutions #7098 (1798.)
[466] Autobiography #7306 (1821.)
[467] To James Barbour #2167 (M., 1812.)
[468] To George Logan #5536 (P.F., Nov. 1816.)
[469] To John Adams #6494 (M., April 1794.)
[470] To Earl of Buchan #6487 (W., 1803.)

powers vested in them, and thereby hang up a rule for the inspection of all, which may direct the conduct of the citizen, and, at the same time, test the judgments they shall themselves pronounce in their own case.[471]

I am not wanting to be accused of Islamophobia, Mr. Jefferson, I want our nation safe. One last fact I want to share with you. Five years ago, the Pew Research Center did a poll[472] and found that 81% of American Muslims thought it was not alright to do suicide bombings or other acts of violence against civilians, to defend Islam from its enemies. If we take out the 6% who did not know if it was alright or not to do suicide bombings, we have 13% left, leaving 429,000 Muslim people in the United States who say suicide bombings and other acts of violence is justified. Scary for America, isn't it.

I feel assured that no American will hesitate to rally round the standard of his insulted country, in defence of that freedom and independence achieved by the wisdom of sages, and consecrated by the blood of heroes.[473]

Mr. Jefferson, that is why this election is the Revolution of 2016. It will be the factor of do we remain a free nation or do we follow Europe into the destruction of their individual nations, with two court structures, with the raping and oppressing of their women, with the enemy living within their

---

[471] Parliamentary Manual #1573
[472] http://www.people-press.org/2011/08/30/muslim-americans-no-signs-of-growth-in-alienation-or-support-for-extremism/
[473] Reply to Georgetown Republicans #6526 (1809.)

countries, always terrorizing, always destroying, always killing; striving to make the sharia law, the law of the land.

*The spirit of our citizens * * * will make this government in practice, what it is in principle, a model for the protection of man in a state of freedom and order.*[474] *The persons and property of our citizens are entitled to the protection of our government in all places where they may lawfully go.*[475]

If we are forced into a war we must give up differences of opinion and unite as one man to defend our country.[476]

God bless America, Mr. Jefferson.

---

[474] To General Kosciusko #7304 (Pa., Feb. 1799.)
[475] Opinion on Ship Passports #7044 (May 1793.)
[476] To General Kosciusko # 8725 (Pa., 1799.)

ON RIGHT TO LIFE

We hold these truths to be self-evident: that all men are created equal; that they are endowed by their Creator with inherent and inalienable rights; that among these are life, liberty and the pursuit of happiness.[477]

They [Indians] raise fewer children than we do. The causes of this are to be found, not in a difference of nature, but of circumstance. The women very frequently attending the men in their parties of war and of hunting, child-bearing becomes extremely inconvenient to them. It is said, therefore, that they have learnt the practice of procuring abortion by the use of some vegetable; and that it even extends to prevent conception for a considerable time after.[478]

---

[477]Declaration of Independence as Drawn by Jefferson #3653 (1776)
[478] Notes on the State of Virginia, Thomas Jefferson, J. W. Randolph 1853, p.65

You are very observant, Mr. Jefferson. As citizens of the United States of America, what do you believe the right to life to be?

The care of human life and happiness, and not their destruction, is the first and only legitimate object of good government.[479] *I sincerely pray that all the members of the human family may, in the time prescribed by the Father of us all, find themselves securely established in the enjoyment of life, liberty and happiness.*[480] *Our rulers can have * * * authority over such natural rights only as we have submitted to them.*[481]

James Wilson, a signer of the Declaration of Independence and the Constitution, and a Supreme Court justice clearly answers this question: "With consistency, beautiful and undeviating, human life from its commencement to its close, is protected by the common law. In the contemplation of law, life begins when the infant is first able to stir in the womb. By the law, life is protected not only from immediate destruction, but from every degree of actual violence, and in some cases, from every degree of danger."[482]

It would * * * be as difficult to say * * * as to fix the moment that the embryo becomes an animal, or the act which gives him a beginning.[483]

---

[479] To Maryland Republicans #3527 (1809.)
[480] Reply to Address #4742 (1807.)
[481] Notes on Virginia #5689 (1782.)
[482] The Works of James Wilson, Associate Justice of the Supreme Court, Edited James DeWitt Andrews, Callaghan and Company, 1895, Vol.2 p.316
[483] To John Adams #7474 (M., 1818.)

Wouldn't it be safe to say then, that life begins at conception. Is it for us to question God's natural right, that of being born?

* * * *those persons, whom nature has endowed with genius and virtue, should be rendered by liberal education worthy to receive, and able to guard the sacred deposit of the rights and liberties of their fellow citizens; and they should be called to that charge without regard to * * * birth, or other accidental condition or circumstance.*[484]

I think it is necessary to guard the sacred deposit of life.

*In a government bottomed on the will of all, the life * * * of every individual citizen becomes interesting to all.*[485]

Plain and simple Mr. Jefferson, abortion is wrong. Some say it is not the government's business.

Good faith ought ever to be the rule of action in public as well as in private transactions.[486] *This, to men of certain ways of thinking, would be to annihilate the blessing of existence, and to contradict the Giver of life, who gave it for happiness and not for wretchedness.*[487]

---

484 Diffusion of Knowledge Bill #836 (1779.)
485 Fifth Annual Message #4745 (1805.)
486 Sixth Annual Message #2855 (1806.)
487 To James Monroe #7605 (M., 1782.)

You got that right. They may grow up to be a leader of our country, or the developer of some great thing, but more importantly, they may grow up to be a mom or dad.

It is in the love of one's family only that heartfelt happiness is known.[488] By a law of our nature, we cannot be happy without the endearing connections of a family.[489] We have reason to value highly the accident of birth in such a one as that of Virginia.[490]

Yes Mr. Jefferson, and this goes for all states as well. It has been proven that family is important. Children do better and are more apt to flourish in a family.

If shame be a powerful affection of the mind, is not parental love also? Is it not the strongest affection known? Is it not greater even than that of self-preservation? Can we change the nature of what is contestable, and make it incontestable? Can we make that conclusive which God and nature have made inconclusive?[491]

The life of a citizen is never to be endangered, but as the last melancholy effort for the maintenance of order and obedience to the laws.[492]

It appears all human life is important to you.

---

[488] To Mary Jefferson Eppes #2867 (W., 1801.)
[489] To W. Clarke #2872 (M., 1809.)
[490] To Martha Jefferson Randolph #1326 (1791.)
[491] Notes To Crime Bill #5574 (1778.)
[492] Circular Letter to State Governors #4752 (W., 1809.)

No crime shall be hence forth punished by the deprivation of life or limb, except those hereinafter ordained to be so punished.[493]

So in your crimes bill, the ordained crimes subject to the deprivation of life were murder and treason. That was quite the reduction from the more than two hundred offences that were punishable by hanging.

No man has a natural right to commit aggression on the equal rights of another; and this is all from which the laws ought to restrain him.[494] *Questions of natural right are triable by their conformity with the moral sense and reason of man.*[495] *Yet we offer adoration to that tutelary God also who rocked the cradle of our birth, who has accepted our infant offerings, and has shown himself the patron of our rights and avenger of our wrongs.*[496]

All things go back to politics, and right to life is no different. The Democrats continue to want to fund a non-governmental business called Planned Parenthood and other organizations. They are in the abortion business and have admitted on camera to selling body parts, a crime in the United States. Once again, the Democrat administration closes their eyes to the injustices. Most of America opposes this. I would guess, if truth be known, about one-third of the Democrats also oppose this. But, the Administration keeps funding; the Congress keeps appropriating the money; and the

---

[493] Crimes Bill #1985 (1779.)
[494] To F. W. Gilmer #5691 (M., 1816.)
[495] Opinion on French Treaties #5693 (1793.)
[496] To Mrs. John Adams #568 (P., 1785.)

Supreme Court continues to overturn the state laws and amendments

To compel a man to furnish contributions of money for the propagation of opinions which he disbelieves and abhors is sinful and tyrannical.[497]

Unfortunately, once again, the Supreme Court and Federal judges do not care about your view, or state laws, as much as their made up story on the "wall of separation," and the liberals desire for abortions.

* * * nor have I ever been able to conceive how any rational being could propose happiness to himself from the exercise of power over others.[498]

---

[497] Statute of Religious Freedom #6272 (1779.)
[498] To M. Destutt Tracy #2814 (M., Jan. 1811.)

ON LIFE IN AMERICA

I shall need the favor of that Being in whose hands we are, Who led our forefathers, as Israel of old, from their native land, and planted them in a country flowing with all the necessaries and comforts of life; Who has covered our infancy with His providence, and our riper years with His wisdom and power; and to whose goodness I ask you to join with me in supplications, that He will so enlighten the minds of your servants, guide their councils, and prosper their measures, that whatsoever they do shall result in your good, and shall secure to you the peace, friendship, and approbation of all nations.[499]

Mr. Jefferson, the prayer still works for today. Let us talk about an array of subjects as we close out our visit. If you have something to bring up, please do so. Sarah Grotjan had

---

[499] Second Inaugural Address #2161 (1805.)

written you twice, once in 1813 concerning an individual, maybe a near relation of the Randolph family; and then in 1824, after the birth of her fifth child, a son named after you. She asked you to write a line or two to her child, which you did.

Your affectionate mother requests that I would address to you, as a namesake, something which might have a favorable influence on the course of life you have to run. Few words are necessary, with good dispositions on your part. Adore God; reverence and cherish your parents; love your neighbor as yourself, and your country more than life. Be just; be true; murmur not at the ways of Providence and the life into which you may have entered will be one of eternal and ineffable bliss. And if to the dead it is permitted to care for the things of this world, every action of your life will be under my regard. Farewell.[500]

What a heartfelt message to a young man you did not know, Mr. Jefferson. Through all your experiences in life, your message is God, family and country. To another young boy, whose father was a friend of yours, you also added more specific information including ten precepts of advice.

Decalogue of Canons for Observation in Practical Life:

   1. *Never put off till to-morrow what you can do to-day.*

---

[500] To Thomas Jefferson Grotjan #162 (M., 1824.)

2. *Never trouble another for what you can do yourself.*
3. *Never spend your money before you have it.*
4. *Never buy what you do not want, because it is cheap; it will be dear to you.*
5. *Pride costs us more than hunger, thirst and cold.*
6. *We never repent of having eaten too little.*
7. *Nothing is troublesome that we do willingly.*
8. *How much pain have cost us the evils which have never happened.*
9. *Take things always by their smooth handle.*
10. *When angry, count ten, before you speak: if very angry, an hundred.*[501]

Great advice Mr. Jefferson. Education was always important to you. One of your greatest achievements and one which you wanted to be remembered, was the founding of the University of Virginia. I find it interesting that we strongly support the Second Amendment. Even with that support, both you and James Madison, and a few others at the 1824 Board of Visitors meeting set a rule, "No student shall, within the precincts of the University, introduce, keep or use any spirituous or vinous liquors, keep or use weapons or arms of any kind, or gunpowder, * * *[502]

A system of general instruction, which shall reach every description of our citizens from the richest to the poorest, as it was the earliest, so will it be the latest of all the public concerns in which I shall permit

---

[501] To Thomas Jefferson Smith #164 (M., 1825.)
[502] University of Virginia Board of Visitors Minutes, October 4-5, 1824, pp6-7, Thomas Jefferson Papers, encyclopediavirginia.org

myself to take an interest. Nor am I tenacious of the form in which it shall be introduced. Be that what it may, our descendants will be as wise as we are, and will know how to amend and amend it, until it shall suit their circumstances. Give it to us then in any shape, and receive for the inestimable boon the thanks of the young and the blessings of the old, who are past all other services but prayers for the prosperity of their country, and blessings for those who promote it.[503]

Unfortunately we are not as wise. We have had bad guidance since the Department of Education was established. I am at fault as so many others. Being young and working for a congressman, I went to the Old Executive Office building for meetings on starting this governmental department. After hearing all the input, I thought it was a good idea and told my Congressman so.

I was wrong and admit it. People generally get smarter with age, hopefully I have. President George Bush started a serious dumbing down of America with the "No Child Left Behind" where children were taught to pass a test, not to think. It was also testing schools, so it forced the schools to teach only to pass the tests, the better the children did on the tests, the better the school did. Then came "Common Core" which, most thinking people find ridiculous.

If it is believed that the elementary schools will be better managed by the Governor and Council, the Commissioners of the Literary Fund, or any other

---

[503] To Joseph C. Cabell #2388 (M., 1818.)

general authority of the government, than by the parents within each ward, it is a belief against all experience.[504]

I agree, the local school boards should run the schools. The local school board should be accountable to the parents for the way the schools should be run.

The reflections that the boys of this age are to be the men of the next; that they should be prepared to receive the holy charge which we are cherishing to deliver over to them; that in establishing an institution of wisdom for them, we secure it to all our future generations; that in fulfilling this duty, we bring home to our own bosoms the sweet consolation of seeing our sons rising under a luminous tuition, to destinies of high promise; these are considerations which will occur to all; but all, I fear, do not see the speck in our horizon which is to burst on us as a tornado, sooner or later. The line of division lately marked out between different portions of our confederacy is such as will never, I fear, be obliterated, and we are now trusting to those who are against us in position and principle, to fashion to their own form the minds and affections of our youth.[505]

I am sure, based on societal changes, you would include young ladies and recognize that our country has made a step forward. Education is now a right for boys and girls, men and

---

[504] To Joseph C. Cabell #7723 (1816.)
[505] To General Breckenridge #8747 (M., 1821.)

women, as women have moved into the workplace alongside men in every facet of our country.

A plan of female education has never been a subject of systematic contemplation with me. It has occupied my attention so far only as the education of my own daughters occasionally required. Considering that they would be placed in a country situation, where little aid could be obtained from abroad, I thought it essential to give them a solid education, which might enable them, when become mothers, to educate their own daughters, and even to direct the course for sons, should their fathers be lost, or incapable, or inattentive.

Women, such as Abigail Adams, and many more of your time, added greatly to the knowledge and common sense, as well as the structure of the United States, which some people found invaluable. John Adams, perhaps, should have listened to her more.

* * * A great obstacle to good education is the ordinate passion prevalent for novels, and the time lost in that reading which should be instructively employed. When this poison infects the mind, it destroys its tone and revolts it against wholesome reading. Reason and fact, plain and unadorned, are rejected. Nothing can engage attention unless dressed in all the figments of fancy, and nothing so bedecked comes amiss. The result is a bloated imagination, sickly judgment, and disgust towards all the real businesses of life. This mass of trash, however, is not without some distinction; some few modelling their narratives, although

fictitious, on the incidents of real life, have been able to make them interesting and useful vehicles of a sound morality.[506]

So you found it important to educate your daughters. I believe you had Martha and Mary sent to a Catholic school, while you lived in France.

It is civilization alone which replaces women in the enjoyment of their natural equality. That first teaches us to subdue the selfish passions, and to respect those rights in others which we value in ourselves.[507]

Now we educate all, and they have the opportunity to work anywhere. We have women as Governors, running for President, and running multinational corporations.

Those who will come after us will be as wise as we are, and as able to take care of themselves as we have been.[508] *Promote in every order of men the degree of instruction proportioned to their condition, and to their views in life.*[509]

Each individual has different talents and abilities, that should be recognized and developed, to better themselves and the country.

I do most anxiously wish to see the highest degrees of education given to the higher degrees of genius, and

---

[506] To N. Burwell #2390 (M., 1818.)
[507] Notes on Virginia #9167 (1782.)
[508] To Dupont de Nemours #3409 (M., 1811.)
[509] To Joseph C. Cabell #2421 (P. F., 1820.)

to all degrees of it, so much as may enable them to read and understand what is going on in the world, and to keep their part of it going on right; for nothing can keep it right but their own vigilant and distrustful superintendence.[510]

So you desire to single out individuals of higher talent and genius. That is not politically correct. You will hurt feelings and some peoples pride. Being politically correct puts people as pegs in the same holes. Differences are ignored, instead of cultivated, allowing each to thrive on their path of life with the talents God gives them. Although I generally agree, some may miss out. One man I know struggled through school, but now is a high paid computer whiz. And then there was Thomas Aquinas, who was referred to as "the Dumb Ox" in his youth. He became a Doctor of the Church and a proponent of natural law. Aquinas became one of the greatest philosophers and theologians, and a Saint. I am surprised you did not have him in your library collection.

Above all things, I hope the education of the common people will be attended to; convinced that on their good senses we may rely with the most security for the preservation of a due degree of liberty.[511] *No other sure foundation can be devised for the preservation of freedom and happiness. * * * Preach a crusade against ignorance; establish and improve the law for educating the common people. Let our countrymen*

---

[510] To Mann Page #2395 (M., 1795.)
[511] To James Madison #2409 (P., 1787.)

know that the people alone can protect us against the evils [of misgovernment].[512]

But what has happened is the teaching of history is not important any more, Mr. Jefferson. According to the educators and the businessmen who do the hiring, science, math and computers is what is necessary and have turned a blind eye to the arts, language, religion, history, ethics and philosophy.

Our laws, language, religion, politics and manners are so deeply laid in English foundations, that we shall never cease to consider their history as a part of ours, and to study ours in that as its origin.[513]

History, by apprising them of the past, will enable them to judge of the future; it will avail them of the experience of other times and other nations; it will qualify them as judges of the actions and designs of men; it will enable them to know ambition under every disguise it may assume; and knowing it, to defeat its views. * * *

Yes and what has become of our political and personal ethics now?

Every government degenerates when trusted to the rulers of the people alone. The people themselves, therefore, are its only safe depositories. And to render even them safe, their minds must be improved to a

---

[512] To George Wythe #2392 (P., 1786.)
[513] To William Duane #3750 (M., 1810.)

certain degree. This indeed is not all that is necessary, though it be essentially necessary.[514]

It is truly unfortunate that those engaged in public affairs so rarely make notes of transactions passing within their knowledge.[515]

Hillary Clinton, as Secretary of State, burned her schedules, taking those records from history. Makes one wonder if it also takes it away from the IRS and the FBI investigation of the Bill, Hillary, and Chelsea Clinton Foundation, too.

College and universities may be found all over the United States, and even on the internet.

I am not a friend to placing young men in populous cities [for their education] because they acquire there habits and partialities which do not contribute to the happiness of their after life.[516]

The biggest crime going on in the United Sates now is the Student Loan Program. The government set up student loans so people could borrow money to go to college. As students started to get the money, then the colleges raised their prices, so students borrow more. Again and again higher education continued to raise their prices as students were able to get more money. Since 1985, the overall consumer price index has risen 115% while the college education inflation rate has risen nearly 500%. [517] When students get out of college, it

---

[514] Notes on Virginia #2400 (1782.)
[515] To William Wirt #3727 (M., 1814.)
[516] To Dr. Wistar #9212 (W., 1807.)
[517] College Costs Out Of Control, Steve Odland, 24 Mar 2012, forbes.com

takes many years to pay the loans off. The default rate is double digits on a nearly 1.4 trillion dollar debt. You promote education, but at what point do you have enough education, so as not to break your rule of, "do not spend before you have the money?" I personally think it is another way the government is getting control of people's lives.

*The greatest good [of the people] requires, that while they are instructed in general, competently to the common business of life, others should employ their genius with necessary information to the useful arts, to inventions for saving labor and increasing our comforts, to nourishing our health, to civil government, military science, &c.[518] If the children * * * are untaught, their ignorance and vices will, in future life cost us much dearer in their consequences, than it would have done, in their correction, by a good education.[519]*

What do you think of English as the national language?

I have been not a little disappointed, and made suspicious of my own judgment, on seeing the Edinburgh Reviews, the ablest critics of the age, set their faces against the introduction of new words into the English language; they are particularly apprehensive that the writers of the United States will adulterate it. Certainly so great growing a population, spread over such an extent of country, with such a variety of climates, of productions, of arts, must enlarge their

---

[518] To Joseph C. Cabell #2396 (P. F., 1820.)
[519] To Joseph C. Cabell #2406 (1818.)

language, to make it answer its purpose of expressing all ideas, the new as well as the old.

The new circumstances under which we are placed, call for new words, new phrases, and for the transfer of old words to new objects. An American dialect will therefore be formed; * * * and should the language of England continue stationary, we shall probably enlarge our employment of it, until its new character may separate it in name as well as in power, from the mother-tongue.[520]

Well, I generally call it American, and my granddaughter corrects me to say English.

We can no longer be called Anglo-Americans. That appellation now describes only the inhabitants of Nova Scotia, Canada, &c. I had applied that of Federo-Americans to our citizens, as it would not be so decent for us to assume to ourselves the flattering appellation of free Americans.[521]

Well good news Mr. Jefferson, we may speak English, but we are proud and free Americans. Some try to hyphenate something with it, but they are wrong. Either they are Americans, citizens of the United States of America. Or they are something else.

Looking at something a little more seriously, Congress has declared war eleven times, the War of 1812; the Mexican War,

---

[520] Thomas Jefferson to John Waldo, LOC August 16, 1813
   http://hdl.loc.gov/loc.mss/mtj.mtjbib020982
[521] To M. de Warville #8721

1846; the War with Spain, 1898; the War with Germany, 1917; The War with Austria-Hungary, 1917; War with Japan, 1941; War with Germany, 1941; War with Italy, 1941; War with Bulgaria, 1942; War with Hungary, 1942; and the War with Rumania, 1942.

Whatever enables us to go to war, secures our peace.[522]

Since WWII, we have had more than a hundred and fifty thousand Americans killed in actions in which Congress has not declared war. We had less than five thousand military deaths in the Revolution. Without Congress declaring war, should soldiers be sent to foreign nations to fight?

If the case were important enough to require reprisal, and ripe for that step, Congress must be called on to take it; the right of reprisal being expressly lodged with them by the Constitution, and not with the Executive.[523] *The question of war, being placed by the Constitution with the Legislature alone, respect to that made it my duty to restrain the operations of our militia to those merely defensive; and considerations involving the public satisfaction, and peculiarly my own, require that the decision of that question, whichever way it be, should be pronounced definitely by the Legislature themselves.*[524]

We have already given, in example, one effectual check to the dog of war, by transferring the power of declaring war from the Executive to the legislative

---

[522] To James Monroe #8923 (N.Y., 1790.)
[523] Opinion on the "Little Sarah" #7291 (1793.)
[524] Paragraph for President's Message #8909 (1792.)

body, from those who are to spend to those who are to pay. I should be pleased to see this second obstacle [that no generation shall contract debts greater than may be paid during the course of its own existence], held out by us also, in the first instance.[525]

Eighteen year olds are now allowed to vote, before the constitutional amendment, voters had to be twenty-one. I believe that came about because of the young soldiers fighting for our country.

Let every man who fights or pays, exercise his just and equal right in the election of [members of the Legislature].[526]

What do you believe of the responsibility of the news in the United States?

No government ought to be without censors; and where the press is free, no one ever will.[527] *[However], the abuses of the freedom of the press here have been carried to a length never before known or borne by any civilized nation.*[528]

The news media seems to be basically in lock step with the left thinking liberals and the Democrat Party. There are some more conservative channels, such as some religious media, such as EWTN, the internet, the radio talk shows and Fox News to some extent. "News" is mostly opinions any more.

[525] To James Madison #8905 (P., 1789.)
[526] To Samuel Kerchival #7276 (M., 1816.)
[527] To President Washington #3477 (M., 1792.)
[528] To M. Pictet #5922 (W., 1803.)

To try to get unbiased news, we have to do some research ourselves. Because we value the truth. You have heard how truthful presidential candidate Hillary Clinton has been, do we believe her that America did not pay $400 million for some hostages in Iran, or do you believe the Iranians, who say it was for the hostages. Knowing Clinton, you would believe someone you do not know, because you know she lies. How can she serve as President?

*A coalition of sentiments is not for the interest of the printers. They, * * *, live by the zeal they can kindle, and the schisms they can create. It is contest of opinion in politics: which makes us take great interest in them, and bestow our money liberally on those who furnish aliment to our appetite.*[529]

We have 24 hour news now, that the media must fill with something, so the media tries to create issues for our appetite. The truth and unbiased reporting, that the world famous journalism school at the University of Missouri was once well known for, now seems to have gone to sensational journalism. Opinions that keep us from the whole truth. Pushing their agendas to sell "news." Research is gone, what one news agency says, is mimicked by many, with no regards to if it is true or not.

The real extent of the misinformation is known only to those who are in situations to confront facts within their knowledge with the lies of the day.[530]

[529] To Elbridge Gerry #2379 (W., March 1801.)
[530] To John Norvell #5941 (W., 1807.)

Perhaps an editor might begin a reformation some such way as this: Divide his paper into four chapters, heading the first "Truths"; the second, "Probabilities"; third, "Possibilities"; fourth, "Lies". The first chapter would be very short, as it would contain little more than authentic papers, and information from such sources, as the editor would be willing to risk his own reputation for their truth. The second would contain what, from a mature consideration of all circumstances, his judgment should conclude to be probably true. This, however, should rather contain too little than too much. The third and fourth should be professedly for those readers who would rather have lies for their money than the blank paper they would occupy.[531]

That is a little harsh Mr. Jefferson, you sound as if the media made personal attacks against you.

As to the volume of slanders supposed to have been cut out of newspapers and preserved [by me] it would not, indeed, have been a single volume, but an encyclopedia in bulk. But I never had such a volume; indeed, I rarely thought those libels worth reading, much less preserving and remembering.[532]

It is really a most afflicting consideration, that it is impossible for a man to act in any office for the public

---

[531] To John Norvell #5971 (W., 1807.)
[532] To John Adams #7925 (M., 1823.)

without encountering a persecution which even his retirement will not withdraw him from.[533]

Welcome to 2016. It is not much better for you. As you are aware of the "news" printed in a newspaper during your election of you having children of a slave, Sally Hemings. There is DNA to tie it to, maybe not you, but to your family.

Were I to undertake to answer the calumnies of the newspapers, it would be more than all my own time, and that of twenty aids could effect. For while I should be answering one, twenty new ones would be invented. I have thought it better to trust to the justice of my countrymen, that they would judge me by what they see of my conduct on the stage where they have placed me, and what they knew of me before the epoch since which a particular party has supposed it might answer some view of theirs to villify me in the public eye. Some, I know, will not reflect how apocryphal is the testimony of enemies so palpably betraying the views with which they give it. But this is an injury to which duty requires every one to submit whom the public think proper to call into its councils.[534]

I believe J. T. Callender, a political trickster, once your acquaintance, accused you of fathering with a slave after you did not make him the postmaster of Richmond.

He knows nothing of me which I am not willing to declare to the world myself.[535] *It is so difficult to draw*

---

[533] To James Monroe #7922 (Pa., 1798.)
[534] To Samuel Smith #1073 (M., 1798.)
[535] To James Monroe #1067 (W., May 1801.)

a clear line of separation between the abuse and the wholesome use of the press, that as yet we have found it better to trust the public judgment, than the magistrate, with the discrimination between truth and falsehood.[536]

The large share I have enjoyed, and still enjoy of anti-republican hatred and calumny, gives me the satisfaction of supposing that I have been some obstacle to anti-republican designs; and if truth should find its way into history, the object of these falsehoods and calumnies will render them honorable to me.[537]

The statue in the photo on the cover of this book oftentimes has post-it notes saying racist and slave owner, or has you completely covered. I know you did much to try to end slavery.

My opinion has ever been that, until more can be done for them, we should endeavor, with those whom fortune has thrown on our hands, to feed and clothe them well, protect them from ill usage, require such reasonable labor only as is performed voluntarily by freemen, and be led by no repugnances to abdicate them, and our duties to them. The laws do not permit us to turn them loose, if that were for their good; and to commute them for other property is to commit them to those whose usage of them we cannot control.[538]

They say you could have freed your slaves to set an example.

---

536 To M. Pictet #5972 (W., 1803.)
537 To W. Lambert #1076 (M., May 1809.)
538 To Edward Coles #7956 (M., 1814.)

I am miserable till I shall owe not a shilling. The moment that shall be the case, I shall feel myself at liberty to do something for the comfort of my slaves.[539]

You did work hard to stop slavery. The first being the stopping of the importation of slaves in Virginia.

This abomination must have an end. And there is a superior bench reserved in heaven for those who hasten it.[540] The abolition of the evil is not impossible; it ought never, therefore, to be despaired of. Every plan should be adopted, every experiment tried, which may do something towards the ultimate object.[541]

This subject was not acted on finally until the year '78, when I brought in a bill to prevent their further importation. This passed without opposition, and stopped the increase of the evil by importation, leaving to future efforts its final eradication.[542]

In 1784, you were the chairman of a committee in Congress, presenting a bill to not allow slavery nor involuntary servitude in the Northwest Territory. In addition it would have included areas which became Alabama Kentucky, Mississippi and Tennessee.

The clause respecting slavery was lost by an individual vote only.[543] There were ten States present; six voted unanimously for it, three against it, and one

---

539 To Nicholas Lewis #7955 (P., 1786.)
540 To E. Rutledge #7935 (P., 1787.)
541 To Miss Fanny Wright #7934 (M., 1825.)
542 Autobiography #7942 (1821.)
543 To James Madison #7929 (A., April 25, 1784.)

*was divided; and seven votes being requisite to decide
the proposition affirmatively, it was lost. The voice of
a single individual of the State which was divided or
of one of those which were of the negative, would
have prevented this abominable crime from spreading itself over the new country. Thus we see the fate
of millions unborn hanging on the tongue of one man,
and heaven was silent in that awful moment! But it is
to be hoped it will not always be silent, and that the
friends to the rights of human nature will in the end
prevail.[544]*

In 1807, as President you signed a bill outlawing the importation of slaves in the United States. You tried many times to
end slavery, even in the proposed Virginia Constitution in 1776.

*I had always hoped that the younger generation
receiving their early impressions after the flame of
liberty had been kindled in every breast, and had
become, as it were, the vital spirit of every American,
that the generous temperament of youth, analogous
to the motion of the blood, and above the suggestions
of avarice, would have sympathized with oppression
wherever found, and proved their love of liberty
beyond their own share of it.[545]*

It would be another thirty-five years after your death, when
the country divided, and a great War between the States was
fought over "States Rights," which included slavery. President
Lincoln emancipated the slaves in the South in 1863, and

---

544 To M. de Meunier #7930 (P., 1786.)
545 To Edward Coles #7947 (M., 1814.)

then the 13th Amendment, ratified in December of 1865, abolished slavery in all of the United States. More than 620,000 American soldiers died in the Civil War. It all may have ended with that one vote, and the United States would be different today.

You ask what all of this has to do with modern day issues, some Blacks continue to blame slavery for their lives.

I am not bigotted to the practices of our forefathers. It is that bigotry which keeps the Indians in a state of barbarism in the midst of the arts, would have kept us in the same state even now.[546]

The Indians, still live mostly on reservations. You hoped for something different.

The ultimate point of rest and happiness for them is to let our settlements and theirs meet and blend together, to intermix, and become one people. Incorporating themselves with us as citizens of the United States, this is what the natural progress of things will of course bring on, and it will be better to promote than to retard it.[547]

The Indians chose your earlier way of doing things.

The most economical as well as the most humane conduct towards them is to bribe them into peace, and to retain them in peace by eternal bribes.

---

[546] To Robert Fulton #352 (M., 1810.)
[547] To Benjamin Hawkins #3899 (1803.)

And there we find them, on reservations. Some of the Cherokee assimilated and had slaves, farms, plantations and mills, but gold was found on their lands. Georgia had land lotteries giving their land away. The Cherokee beat Georgia in the United States Supreme Court, but Jackson did not support it. President Andrew Jackson and the State of Georgia shipped them by way of the Trail of Tears to Oklahoma.

The foundation on which all [our constitutions] are built, is the natural equality of man, the denial of every pre-eminence but that annexed to legal office and, particularly, the denial of a pre-eminence by birth.[548]

All of this leads up to a group called Black Lives Matter, supported by the liberal left, President Obama, Hillary Clinton and the Democrat Party. They call them Black activists for civil rights who want us to believe they represent all Black Americans. Not true. Seems to me that God created us and all lives matter.

It is a singular anxiety which some people have that we should all think alike. Would the world be more beautiful were all our faces alike? Were our tempers, our talents, our tastes, our forms, our wishes, aversions and pursuits cast exactly in the same mould? If no varieties existed in the animal, vegetable or mineral creation, but all moved strictly uniform, catholic and orthodox, what a world of physical and moral monotony would it be. These are the absurdities into which those run who usurp the throne of God, and

[548] To General Washington #354 (A., 1784.)

dictate to Him what He should have done. May they with all their metaphysical riddles appear before that tribunal with as clean hands and hearts as you and I shall. There, suspended in the scales of eternal justice, faith and works will show their worth by their weight.[549]

Unfortunately our welfare laws, as discussed earlier has kept all of the poor American's down for the last 60 years. Fifty-eight percent of the Black youth are unemployed because of poor trade agreements and immigration laws. Presidential candidate Donald Trump has said that his economic programs will help correct this problem. Each and every person can promote and be responsible for family, love, and education. These expectations will go a long way into correcting the problems which plague our nation. These should be supported by every American.

*Every human being must thus be viewed, according to what it is good for; for none of us, no not one, is perfect; and were we to love none who had imperfections, this world would be a desert for our love. All we can do is to make the best of our friends, love and cherish what is good in them, and keep out of the way of what is bad; * * * Let no proof be too much for either your patience or acquiescence. Be you the link of love, union, and peace for the whole family.*[550]

Instead of these values, the group which been infiltrated with hate and terrorists gangs, has called for the killing of our

---

[549] To Charles Thomson #8648 (M., 1817.)
[550] To Martha Jefferson Randolph #2865 (N.Y.,1790.)

police, the killing of whites, and rioting. Although most Black Americans are not part of this movement, they are now becoming entwined with it by the media, causing hate, fear and confusion. Telling the people that only Black Lives Matter instead of mending the issues and rifts. They have also become paid protesters for Democrat operatives.

While the principles of our Constitution give just latitude to inquiry, every citizen faithful to it will deem embodied expressions of discontent, and open outrages of law and patriotism, as dishonorable as they are injurious.[551]

It is unfortunate that there is more racism now, then when President Obama was elected as the first Black President. He has promoted it with events such as in Ferguson, Missouri. It seems that with thirteen percent of America being Black, Obama being elected would show that racism was down in America. Rioting and killing does not support the cause.

Single acts of tyranny may be ascribed to the accidental opinion of a day; but a series of oppressions, begun at a distinguished period, and pursued unalterably through every change of ministers, too plainly prove a deliberate, systematical plan of reducing us.[552]

The property destruction is great, and the killings continue. The leaders of the Democrat Party and the President encourage the

---

[551] To Leesburg Citizens #4515 (1809.)
[552] Rights of British America #8642 (1774.)

group, with the Democrat National Committee passing a resolution in support of the movement.

The Great Spirit did not make men that they might destroy one another, but doing to each other all the good in their power, and thus filling the land with happiness instead of misery and murder.[553] The friends of reform, while they remain firm, [should] avoid every act and threat against the peace of the Union. That would check the favorable sentiments of the middle States, and rally them again around the measures which are ruining us. Reason, not rashness, is the only means of bringing our fellow citizens to their true minds.[554]

There has always been religious zealots who have been calling for the end of the world. The same as you hear now. My Mother, visiting cousins, when she was a child, found them all in bed, waiting for the end of the world, as was predicted at that time.

I hope you will have good sense enough to disregard those foolish predictions that the world is to be at an end soon. The Almighty has never made known to anybody at what time He created it; nor will He tell anybody when He will put an end to it, if He ever means to do it.

As to preparations for that event, the best way for you is to be always prepared for it. The only way to

---

553 Indian Address #4966 (1809.)
554 To N. Lewis #3058 (1799.)

be so is, never to say or do a bad thing. If ever you are about to say anything amiss, or to do anything wrong, consider beforehand you will feel something within you which will tell you it is wrong, and ought not to be said or done. This is your conscience, and be sure and obey it.

Our Maker has given us all this faithful internal monitor, and if you always obey it you will always be prepared for the end of the world; or for a much more certain event, which is death. This must happen to all; it puts an end to the world as to us; and the way to be ready for it is never to do a wrong act.[555] *We often repent of what we have said, but never of that which we have not.*[556]

Mr. Jefferson, it is getting time to close out, it has been enlightening and inspiring to learn from you. You have given us so much to think about. We have spent this time talking of our great nation, how about a few words of wisdom for the lives of those reading of you.

Truth can stand by itself.[557] *I do believe we shall continue to grow, to multiply and prosper until we exhibit an association, powerful, wise and happy beyond what has yet been seen by men.*[558] *We are not in a world ungoverned by the laws and the power of a Superior Agent. Our efforts are in His hand, and*

---

[555] To Martha Jefferson #9172 (1783.)
[556] To Gideon Granger #7900 (M., 1814.)
[557] Notes on Virginia #3502 (1782.)
[558] To John Adams #8707 (M., 1812.)

directed by it; and He will give them their effect in His own time.[559]

*Of all exercises walking is the best. * * * No one knows, till he tries, how easily a habit, of walking is acquired. A person who never walked three miles will in the course of a month become able to walk fifteen or twenty without fatigue. I have known some great walkers, and had particular accounts of many more; and I never knew or heard of one who was not healthy and long lived.*[560]

As to the species of exercise, I advise the gun. While this gives a moderate exercise to the body, it gives boldness, enterprise, and independence to the mind. Games played with ball, and others of that nature, are too violent for the body, and stamp no character on the mind. Let your gun, therefore, be the constant companion of your walks.[561] *One loves to possess arms, though they hope never to have occasion for them.*[562]

Determine never to be idle. No person will have occasion to complain of the want of time who never loses any. It is wonderful how much may be done, if we are always doing.[563]

Thank you Mr. Jefferson. You have given me and many others much to pause and think about.

---

[559] To David Barrow #2154 (M., 1815.)
[560] To T. M Randolph, Jr. #2829 (P., 1786.)
[561] To Peter Carr #2820 (P., 1785.)
[562] To President Washington #2138 (M., 1796.)
[563] To Martha Jefferson #8444 (Mar. 1787.)

When we assemble together to consider the state of our beloved country, our just attentions are first drawn to those pleasing circumstances which mark the goodness of that Being from whose favor they flow, and the large measure of thankfulness we owe for His bounty.[564]

I offer my sincere prayers to the Supreme Ruler of the Universe, that He may long preserve our country in freedom and prosperity.[565]

As a great American, who also cared about what happened across the globe, I give you the last word.

I wish that all nations may recover and retain their independence; that those which are overgrown may not advance beyond safe measures of power, that a salutary balance may be ever maintained among nations, and that our peace, commerce and friendship, may be sought and cultivated by all.[566]

---

[564] Second Annual Message #2149 (Dec. 1802.)
[565] To Benjamin Waring #2155 (W., March 1801.)
[566] To Thomas Leiper #5643 (M., 1815.)

#xxx The Jeffersonian Encyclopedia, Edited by John P. Foley, Copyright 1900, by Funk & Wagnalls Company.

33. Thomas Jefferson to John Cartwright, June 5, 1824. -06-05, 1824. Manuscript/Mixed Material. Retrieved from the Library of Congress, <https://www.loc.gov/item/mtjbib025031/>.

74. Thomas Jefferson to Joseph Milligan, April 6, 1816. -04-06, 1816. Manuscript/Mixed Material. Retrieved from the Library of Congress, <https://www.loc.gov/item/mtjbib022403/>.

91. Thomas Jefferson to William Johnson, June 12, 1823. -06-12, 1823. Manuscript/Mixed Material. Retrieved from the Library of Congress, <https://www.loc.gov/item/mtjbib024682/>.

92. Madison, James, and Thomas Jefferson. Thomas Jefferson to James Madison, December 20, 1787. 1787. Manuscript/Mixed Material. Retrieved from the Library of Congress, <https://www.loc.gov/item/mjm023176/>.

98. Thomas Jefferson to William Johnson, June 12, 1823. -06-12, 1823. Manuscript/Mixed Material. Retrieved from the Library of Congress, <https://www.loc.gov/item/mtjbib024682/>.

154. Thomas Jefferson to George Washington, May 16, 1792. -05-16, 1792. Manuscript/Mixed Material. Retrieved from the Library of Congress, <https://www.loc.gov/item/mtjbib006165/>.

179. American Peace Commissioners to John Jay, March 28, 1786. -03-28, 1786. Manuscript/Mixed Material. Retrieved from the Library of Congress, <https://www.loc.gov/item/mtjbib001849/>.

258. Justice Clarence Thomas No. 15–274. Argued March 2, 2016—Decided June 27, 2016 <https://www.supremecourt.gov/opinions/15pdf/15-274_p8k0.pdf>.

286. Thomas Jefferson to George Washington, February 15, 1791, Opinion on Bill for Establishing a National Bank. -02-15, 1791. Manuscript/Mixed Material. Retrieved from the Library of Congress, <https://www.loc.gov/item/mtjbib005219/>.

290. Thomas Jefferson to David Humphreys, January 20, 1809. -01-20, 1809. Manuscript/Mixed Material. Retrieved from the Library of Congress, <https://www.loc.gov/item/mtjbib019612/>.

299. Ibid.

387. Robert Frank, Top 1% Pay Nearly Half of Federal Income Taxes, CNBC, 14 Apr. 2015 <http://www.cnbc.com/2015/04/13/top-1-pay-nearly-half-of-federal-income-taxes.html>.

389. Jillian Kay Melchior, The Ten Most Ridiculous Ways the Government Wastes Your Money, National Review, 02 Dec 2015, <http://www.nationalreview.com/article/427891/top-10-wasteful-government-expenses>.

390. Federal Fumbles, Senator James Lankford, <https://www.lankford.senate.gov/imo/media/doc/Federal_Fumbl es_2015.pdf>.

406. US Tax Center, Tax Preparation Costs and Fees, <https://www.irs.com/articles/tax-preparation-costs-and-fees>.

414. Thomas Jefferson to William Canby, September 18, 1813. -09-18, 1813. Manuscript/Mixed Material. Retrieved from the Library of Congress, <https://www.loc.gov/item/mtjbib021517/>.

430. Library of Congress, Religion and the Founding of the American Republic Religion and the Federal Government, Part 2, The State Becomes the Church: Jefferson and Madison, <https://www.loc.gov/exhibits/religion/rel06-2.html>.

437. Thomas Jefferson to Benjamin Rush, April 21, 1803, with Syllabus of an Estimate of the Merit of the Doctrines of Jesus, with Copies; Partial Transcription Available. -04-21, 1803. Manuscript/Mixed Material. Retrieved from the Library of Congress, <https://www.loc.gov/item/mtjbib012336/>.

440. Ibid. 180.

444. Stoyan Zaimov, ISIS Horror: 19 Girls Burned Alive in Iron Cage for Refusing to Have Sex With Terror Group, CP World, <http://www.christianpost.com/news/isis-horror-19-girls-burned-alive-iron-cage-refusing-sex-terror-group-164913/>.

461. Besheer Mohamed, A New Estimate of the U.S. Muslim Population, PewResearchCenter, January 6, 2016,<http://www.pewresearch.org/fact-tank/2016/01/06/a-new-estimate-of-the-u-s-muslim-population/>.

462. Center for Security Policy, Poll of U.S. Muslims Reveals Ominous Levels Of Support For Islamic Supremacists' Doctrine of Shariah, Jihad, <http://www.centerforsecuritypolicy.org/2015/06/23/nationwide-poll-of-us-muslims-shows-thousands-support-shariah-jihad/>.

472. Muslim Americans: No Signs of Growth in Alienation or Support for Extremism, PewResearchCenter, August 30, 2011, <http://www.people-press.org/2011/08/30/muslim-americans-no-signs-of-growth-in-alienation-or-support-for-extremism/>.

478. Notes on the State of Virginia, Thomas Jefferson, J. W. Randolph, 1853, p.65.

482. The Works of James Wilson, Associate Justice of the Supreme Court, Edited James DeWitt Andrews, Callaghan and Company, 1895, Vol.2 p.316

502. Encyclopedia Virginia, University of Virginia Board of Visitors Minutes, October 4-5, 1824, pp6-7, Thomas Jefferson Papers, <http://www.encyclopediavirginia.org/University_of_Virginia_Board_of_Visitors_Minutes_October_4-5_1824>.

517. Steve Odland, College Costs Out Of Control, 24 Mar 2012, forbes.com, <http://www.forbes.com/sites/steveodland/2012/03/24/college-costs-are-soaring/#202c9048641b>.

520. Thomas Jefferson to John Waldo, August 16, 1813. -08-16, 1813. Manuscript/Mixed Material. Retrieved from the Library of Congress, <https://www.loc.gov/item/mtjbib020982/>.

Back Cover Lincoln Quote   Complete Works of Abraham Lincoln, Vol. 1, Edited by Nicolay & Hay, The Century Co. 1894, pp532-33.

ABOUT THE AUTHOR

Clifford Olsen is a Certified Financial Planner, CFP®, who has been involved in the insurance and securities business since the late 1980's. He graduated from the University of Missouri-Columbia with degrees in Economics, Public Administration and Political Science.

Clifford has always been involved in politics, first going to Washington, D.C. to work when he was eighteen. Starting as a Democrat, then evolving into a Republican, and now a Conservative without ever changing his basic beliefs.

Clifford studies the history of America, often times through his genealogical work. He is a member of the Sons of the American Revolution, the Boy Scouts of America, Firehouse Woodcarvers and the Masonic Lodge. His views do not represent any of the organizations he is affiliated.

Made in the USA
Lexington, KY
15 October 2016